WAR AND PEACE

volume *4*

Vision *and* Text

Edited by Judith Goldman and Leslie Scalapino

O *Books* • Oakland • 2009

Front cover: Susan Bee, *Diving into the Wreck*, 2005, oil and collage on linen, 52 x 68 inches

Back cover: Petah Coyne, *Untitled #1240 (Black Cloud)*, 2007-08, silk flowers, silk/rayon velvet, plaster statuary, feathers, specially formulated wax, cable, cable nuts, acrylic paint, black spray paint, plaster, chicken wire fencing, metal hardware, felt, pearl-headed hat pins, pigment, thread, wire, plywood, wood, 74 x 104 x 174 inches (188 x 264.2 x 442 cm), © Petah Coyne, Courtesy Galerie Lelong, New York

Cover and book design: Amy Evans McClure

The editors would like to thank Coffee House Press for the republication of "Isle of the Signatories," from *Isle of the Signatories* (2008) by Marjorie Welish.

We thank Granary Books for allowing us to print from color spreads of images and text from *Oaths? Questions?* (2009) by Marjorie Welish and James Siena.

We thank Granary Books for allowing us to print from color spreads of images and text from *The Animal is in the World like Water in Water* (2009) by Leslie Scalapino and Kiki Smith.

We thank the publisher for two pages from Jenny Boully's *The Body: An Essay*. Slope Editions (Buffalo, NY), 2002, 1st ed. Essay Press (Athens, OH), 2007, 2nd ed.

ISBN # 1-882022-68-8
$15.00

O Books
5744 Presley Way
Oakland, CA 94618
www.obooks.com

Contents

Petah Coyne

Black Cloud

Petah Coyne described the sculpture in her show *Vermilion Fog* (a collection of works shown at Galerie Lelong in New York, fall 2008) as her interior narrative of Dante, Beatrice, and Virgil in works that are as if landscapes of the *Inferno*, scenes also associated with Clint Eastwood's film *Unforgiven*. The works contain real birds that were stuffed by a conservation reserve, flowers covered in wax; in one piece, the figure of Virgil appears as a stuffed bobcat. The work titled "Black Cloud" (above and back cover) 'contains' the figure of Beatrice flowing at the head of a train of flowers that as if flowing covered in wax are terrain of ascending-descending (stuffed, real) birds. Coyne commented to me that the weight of our actions seems in some cases so heavy as not to allow forgiveness. Ann Wilson Lloyd, in an essay for the catalogue titled "Dark Night at Heart's Lake" (*Vermilion Fog*, Galerie LeLong, New York, 2008, p. 17), quotes Coyne: "Dante's *Inferno* is very much about the personal and the public, what happens to all of us. The imagery is so beautiful, the descent into the concentric circles, all those trapdoors. Each soul appears, tells his or her own individual story and dives back into their own dark hole." Lloyd comments: "In the fourteenth century, men of science ascribed the flow of unbridled passions, fear and anxiety, to an actual source in the human heart called the 'heart's lake.'"

— *Leslie Scalapino*

Kiki Smith and Leslie Scalapino

FROM *The Animal is in the World like Water in Water*

is there any way

there is no higher or
lower
so one is by
the animal is in the
world like water in water?

how
[can]
do
we
have
any
relation

to

any
thing to be
neither
higher nor
lower
than

anything

else?

then
anything
outside is

Or

if the girl

pours praise on some *one*

meaning what she says—of one
who'd only
flattered everyone to
elicit praise

then the girl meaning it separate, alone

is in the world like water in water
[alongside beside by the animal]?

How can that be alone: [like water in
water]?

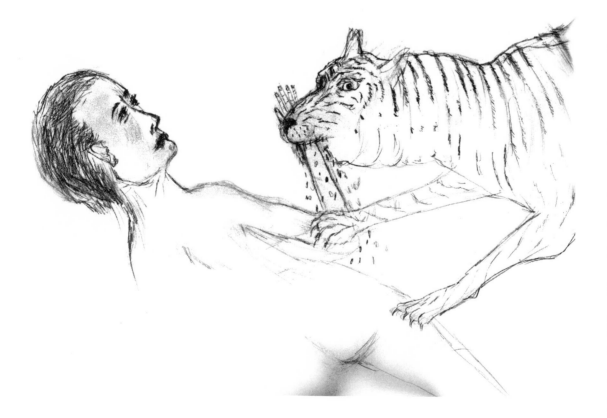

capacity
of speaking, though silent

no ascendancy

and animal girl by them

her thoughts are not

separating the ivory night [the night not there yet *then*]

next to by beside the night—both
yet there are blooms [there—but not seen]

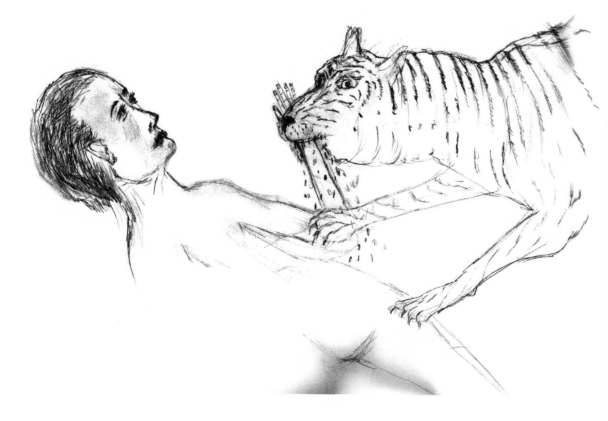

tears come out

they appear

red flecked—though the animal

scratched day light

on her face pouring—tears—

someone she'd

praised, her meaning it
                       the other
scoffs at tears being expressed inside beside by ivory day
                              that's retaining ascendancy
in which she's confronted by that mad person unseen

the one who has only power

the animal makes

holes in

the girl—the night [not there yet]

is

[night] in the same place then

as both—and holes in night where're
stars seen [by them their inside it]?

where're

stars?

she sees stars

not there

when the animal bites her hand

then

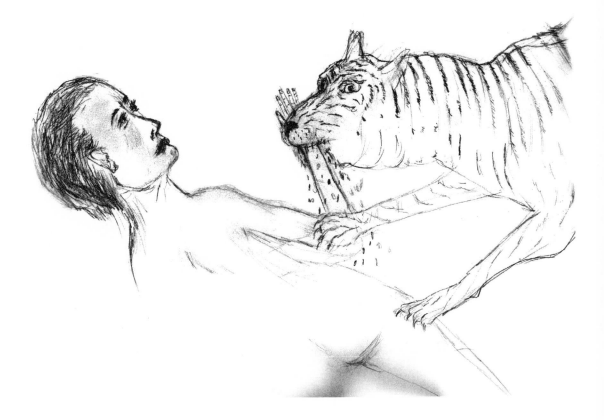

what it

many

people

want

authority?

she *doesn't*

[doesn't want it]

[is no ascendancy]

Leslie Scalapino

The Division Between Fact and Experience

The Animal is in the World like Water in Water is a collaboration of drawings by Kiki Smith and poetry by Leslie Scalapino (myself), published by Granary Books in 2009. Kiki Smith sent me color Xeroxes of a completed sequence, forty-three drawings, which she'd titled *Women Being Eaten by Animals*. I wrote the poem using the sense of an unalterable past occurrence: One female, apparently the same girl, is repeatedly, in very similar images as variations, bitten and clawed by a leopard-like, lion-like animal. Both person and animal have abstracted features, giving the impression of innocence or opaqueness. As in a dream of similar actions or a dream of a single, timeless action, the girl flecked with blood while being unaltered by the animal's touch, there is no representation of motion except stillness of the figures floating in space of page. Neither the girl, nor the animal articulate expression, as if phenomena of feeling(s) do not exist.

Each of my poems (in my sequence) corresponds to a particular image of Kiki's sequence, my intention being that the two sequences (vision and text) would co-exist at once yet be separate, having a double title: *The Animal is in the World like Water in Water/Women Being Eaten by Animals*. The two realities, or two views of the fact of the actual occurrence, are side by side. My title is a phrase from George Bataille's *The Theory of Religion*, a phrase he repeats as a poetic riff throughout his essay. My use of Kiki's title as a double (her title was later dropped from the Granary book) was intentionally redundant: the visual will dominate the viewer/reader's perception. The fact of women being eaten by animals, or of one woman being eaten by one animal that sometimes changes appearance (again, as in a dream), will seem to the viewer to be the primary, if not the *only*, real experience or true interpretation of the experience. Thus the double title would highlight the division between fact and experience. Absent, the double title is still implied (maybe more compellingly?).

The poem's present-time (sometimes a single word is a line, or *part* of a phrase is a line that as such alters the action of that phrase as it unfolds on other lines/presents-of-time) is to render the sense that 'the word' abuts sensory space that is of (in) the world. That is, 'the word,' as spatial, *also* makes a sense of sensory space, in relation to and different from the space of the visual world. 'The word' in *its* outside/space refers to and makes a sense of the undoing of social tyranny as undoing of *any* hierarchy in individuals' feelings and perception as well as in people's values (public indistinguishable from private). Without hierarchy, past-reality-future is apparently free paradise of childhood and of birds. 'This outside space of the word/or that is the word' abuts the other visible space of "Women being eaten by animals" (that original title of the visual images denied, however, by the fact that the female figure appears to be almost a child). The visual scene itself is denied by 'not experiencing.' The viewer (while reading beside seeing the images, but also if only seeing the visual images?) has the experience of body and mind being separated as if that is *caused by* the outside world. This experience of the viewer arises from their sense, *in seeing*, that one is separated from the scene of the girl and the animal alone together as if making love (and a sense of separation arises from the girl and animal *not* mimicking expressions of experiencing sensations). The disconnect/that's itself the dialogue between 'not being experienced (by the senses)'— and separation *or* union of mind/eye and body/sight—has to be *first* enacted by Smith's visual images, in order for the language to broach this (subject) matter at all. Is dialogue possible without language?

My poem sequence is to reinstate (restate) experiencing in space, the mind/eye making estimations/approximations as concepts that are the *same* as their being in space: The language makes minute distinctions of its theme and treats these as spatial. For example, the poem-segments posit: society *not* based on emulation, no individual regarded as higher than another; and posit the individual perceiving in such a way— *not* having such feelings or behavior of emulation or sense of immanence—though (the segments posit) the individual is aware that others *do*, different from an animal's view. These concepts *in the world*, however, are not submitted to space. (In the world, concepts of feelings—such as peoples in societies feeling social values, having internalized these—are not submitted to *this* sense of space, of no-hierarchy.) *Here* they are submitted to space (of no-hierarchy) to be translated to (a sense of) free space/shape /place. The format of the Granary book is accordion-like, continuous pages, suggesting a horizontal scroll, in that figures on a page are complete yet an extension of a limb or body on one page may appear to overlap on the next page, giving the impression that we are seeing alteration occurring in a repeated scene (or: origination *in one similar*). This horizontal non/narrative, as apparent overlap of images in continuous connection/action of the same *or similar* figures, read horizontally, is: *not* having hierarchy that would value one individual image above another; nor is there hierarchy of narrative as transpiring event. The language (of poem-segments) approximates a state impossible anywhere except by being *in* one (can't be approximated except experienced by a person).

Abigail Child

FROM War Correspondence

Dramatis Personae

The soldier (He)
The soldier's lover (back home) (She)
The politician
The commander
The lover's friend (back home)
Passers-by

What the soldier said:

Basically we're bullet sponge
Sandbagged and bristling
At bottom of a natural amphitheater deep within

Enemy territory
Cannot hear our grunts
Over the summary

Lights out
Fighting breaks in
No cladding

Redness a sacrifice to metal impact speeding
So fast it seems impossible
Drawing insurgents away

From more populated
Once a hunting lodge for kings
Now littered shattered blown to splinters

Crepuscular smithereens
No proxy to ignore close calls
Parasites night pile

So its red glow does not gorge
In summer's stinking waste

What the soldier's lover said (back home):

Twilight when sounds change
Pack desire's innuendo

What the soldier's lover said (back home):

Twilight when sounds change
Pack desire's innuendo
Landscape replays you

Rescuing my body
As if capacity repelled congruent limit
Pause of air

Mowed heat
Night belongs to each
Recalibrates care

Makes me whisper
Wanting negotiation
Outside menu

Camouflaged by advertisement
Unbewitched clock
Allows sleep

Steep staggering rains
On grassy bank
Near intervallic symphonic jiminy

Slow collide as train goes by
Fears precipitate

What the politician said:

Going forward
Pent up with priorities
The issue of prisoners

Tackling dummies
(And if I might like money
Patronizing nemesis—yes

Study is sparking debate
Study is parking rebates
Studly ark darkening

Behind a lackluster legation
Lacking heart
Occurring in a half-head

Speaking on condition of anonymity
It is running behind
Ethnically mixed neighborhoods

And urges a manifesto for Sunday
Using a status hypothesis
He comments:

Two women and a ten-year-old girl
Were killed yesterday.

What the soldier said:

My ears are bleeding
Briefly illuminated by a
Beautiful bad noise

Floating in darkness of white phosphorous
A one-liner across our face
Filed by routines in a hostile

Latrine
Fed by a pipe
Carrying low-flying reprisals

Insults risk night
And far fewer comforts
To indulge breath

A common and not verifiable rumor
If vampires could clap
They'd be clapping

Name withheld
Moved into place by donkeys
Flak jack pretty decisively

Living the dream
Light breaks

What the politician said:

Listen
And obey laws of arithmetic
This has led to a natural suspicion

Special pleaders
Turn on a dime
No secondhand resurrection

Bounds precedent
Unanalyzable quietism
Uncannily extracted

Who goes hungry watching television?
I mean zygote entitled
Let's do this now

Clincher
(Who also killed) his brother,
His mother and his sister

Scrambling, I need a majority
Tunneling through profit boys
Intrigue contingent

As nation blood places them
Close to our bank

What her friend says:

It's only the beginning
Each face she needs
Trips up her engine

Reads
Discontinuity
On a long horizon

Lupine, wild mustard, poppy
Flies of dusty wings on fire
Vast fields emotion

Each face makes portable
Not so much reversible
As fluid

She's next in line
Packing groceries at the Food Lion
No glass slipper

No grass a sea can't hide
Against wadded smells
Humans decorate their copy

Nothing more insecure
Than waiting

What his commander says:

Dockets crisis tam-tam
A wrong kind of savvy
Stretched by obstruction

He stands to
Violence unsilent
Truth not based on history

But a structure of conception
Undone
Praying internally

First they fire
Come solely overhead and opposite
Rushing

I'm just so tired
Army forbids
Disclosing death's numbers

So we push out and get on
No Oz here
It's certain

The road to the castle costly
Hissed over, watched—drags

What she said:

I miss your long white body
Your legs entwined with mine
Your eyes muddy and kind

Your laugh unexpectedly boyish
Carriage rides
Watch light's passage

Snow naps once red
Now absent
Out of time itself unwound

Talking to self
Ghosts wander wonder
Memory becomes waiting

Corporeal revels
You were (I fear) never here
Your ear heart hands

Not—
No imprint on now's body
Now, let me alone

Thinking of you
Solicitude adoringly photographed

What he said:

By what inhuman calculus
I sweat through fog
Besieged

Recognizing nothing
But scale of ourselves
Every day, every single flight, each

An implacable unrest
We need to be clear
About horrors, doubtful news, fever of automatics

A few dozen armed men
Die uneasily in my memory hole
Ill doing loss

Nearby their arm, my eye
No possible gain
Real or fancied indifference

Of those back home
To go on
Beyond reach of moldy food smell death

Myself apart—
O lucky lie, I deny repress.

What she said:

He has not written
I get right words wrong
Irregular attention inopportune

Unrenewed by kisses
You are not here
Planning my anxiety

Love is absent-minded
Snow thick heavy continuous blocks sight
I see stars at night

And send them caresses
In hopes they fall on you
Laugh in my head bubbling

If only if only—I surrender
To live in any real way is painful
My heart worn forgotten marshalled

I'd like to talk about forgotten things
Curling along your mouth
Summer crickets wile along fences

You are far away
Who can argue?

Susan Bee and Charles Bernstein

Vision in question and response

vision is question and response

VISION IS QUESTION AND RESPONSE

Vision in Motion

thus by ordinate demand
demonstrating the abiding circus of incapacity's
love of reeling rapture in the maimed
vision of circumnavigation's song.

What's the vision and what's the version?

"As a voice in a vision that's vanished."

NOTHING TIRES A VISION MORE THAN SUNDRY ATTACKS

The body-with-only-organs may still be intact *(there's still some time but the planet and those on it are in danger)*; then this dimming of vision *(what I've called "sight")* is something like hysterical, imaginary, but there remains the material organic possibility of ambi-opia--multilevel seeing, which is to say, **vision repossessed.**

The blacktop of the road a vision of Paradise.

Charles Bernstein

Today Is the Last Day of Your Life 'til Now

I was the luckiest father in the world
until I turned unluckiest.
They shoot horses, don't they?
In the mountains, the air is so
Thin you can scarcely say your
name. I dreamt I was a drum.
In the dream, I dreamt I was a
school boy afraid of school. I dreamt
I was drowning. Far away, the
crush of snow refracted the still muted
light. As if punishment was not
punishment enough.

(Jan. 14, 2009)

If You Say Something, See Something

for Emma

It didn't happen that fast
clobbered by the silt of mineral movement
tempted to board the welter
of inspecific media capture
burnt like leers on the sprain.
Cajole me into oblivion if not
obliviousness, clotted clearings that
jam like slate. I didn't
mean to do it—intention
doesn't even enter the equilibrations.
Send me away, I've never been there.

(Dec. 10, 2008)

Amy Evans McClure and Michael McClure

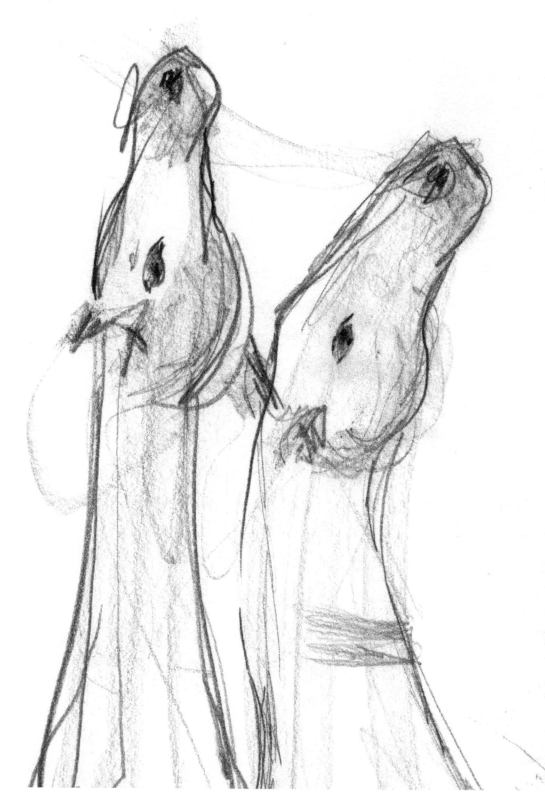

1

IT MAY BE THE WAY OF ALL FLESH
to sense backward through itself:
(ORGANS TISSUES AND SYSTEMS
OF DANCING LOVERS
MAKING CELLS)

and to see the sides and front through
star banks
in the eyes of a sparrow.

2

BEING BORN IS NOTHINGNESS.
DYING IS NOTHINGNESS.
Grandpa and Mama are nothingness
and I am here with
ALL LIVES
I
N
VENTING

a love
— half free.

Coming into being is matter,
passing through is not matter;

in the black deeps
light eats light,
shitting coal.

Marjorie Welish

Isle of the Signatories

1

The following lines were omitted:

Even in Arcady I exist
e-signature in whose writings
lie the body
or its facsimile
Et in arcadia, I also, Pierre
Saw "Pierre" there also.

2

The following lines were omitted:

I, too, have known Arcady
Name, signature
Here lie
Ego's avatars also
I, Jacques Rivière,
The lie:
Fabrication requires a thinker, he said.
Whereas, he went on, attempting to think
Any thought, yet

Attempting to think henceforth
As a text though ex temporare
All were reprinted
With the lyric effect
His and "there is"
By adverting to the effect.

3

The following lines were omitted, probably deliberately:

I, Marni Nixon, unpaginated
—spacing.

And the corrected typescript
At table, as a text
Attempting to think henceforth

To think as the corrected typescript would think
through the lyric effect
incited to rhetoric where structure had been.

Followed by an additional line:

I, writing.

4

Followed by an additional line:

I also dwell in Arcady,
The best signature on the subject
Lightly written yet penetrating signature
Sprightly, fair-minded and comprehensive signature
None has the intellectual and personal authority of this signature:

I also Pierre saw "Pierre."
beneath this stone.

The writing said:

Tempting thought.
Primarily any "irrepressible"
Irrepressibly meant
Spontaneity.
For "poetry" read "lyric"
His and "this" and "Here lies"

Ivy, underappreciated.

5

Don't / Do not. In all printings prior to CEP.
Unnumber
Do not paginate: leave
istoria where structure had been.

I, Jacques Rivière,
Writing.

In an itinerary of identity, I, too,
Ego's avatars also, I, Jacques Rivière,
Am signing my name, relentlessly

6

here interred
is "Pierre"
of the picture plane

it them   it and them
if then   if them
not to mention

someone else
nonempty pagination
it is said here

7

It is said here lie these peoples:

Uncorrected proof
Underpaginated

It them   it and them
Not to mention the counterfactual

Were it the case that
Were it so

Following a different ambidextrous line
That is to say the three broad responses

The three broad responsive
~~The following lines were omitted~~

Probably deleted
Themnpting thought

8

Forgetting
To anticipate, he advocated,
Enables listening to her

Less damning to
Hearing her

Followed by an additional line:

The lyric effect creases the self-evident

Reference
She sang

Followed by an additional line:

I, too, am in Arcady
(signed) Marni Nixon
the unpaginated voice

incited to narrative.
What is narrative?
What is science?

9
(signed)
Marni Nixon, the unpaginated

Voice incited to narrative

His anticipating the identity
Of poetry

What is poetry?

10
Even in Arcady, I (Death) am here
A disputa

And decipherment
She sang

Through other texts
A palette

Of irritability
Constitutive of

A signature—
Her singular voiceprint

Which is to say "I am here"
The competent reader

11
Albeit

ventriloquism
I death even exist here in Arcady

In Situ

HERE LIE
THE FALLEN

Here lie the fallen phrasing s of
exemption and non-exemption

Here lies the fallen phrasing of
commemorative writing on behalf of
exemption and non-exemption
without which and without whom

THIS CERTIFIES THAT

This certifies that writing so named
was completed in accordance with
programmed guy wires with/without
naming undertaken in fact yet

as agreed as described

FOUND

Road under purse allowing the debut of coins
the debit of its mouth

ROAD OPEN
to mouth at or on coins, road rolling under

A lay purse, mouth open, let out a coin
LOST? PLACED?
A coin toss
well-informed as to time, sequence and location

DATED MATERIAL

If you are currently receiving
if you do not receive
valid through
validate by

a lingering taste

Of discursive space the color of substrate: Start
from rent: THIS IS A NON-EVICTION PLAN
NO NON-RESIDENTIAL PURCHASING TENANT
WILL BE EVICTED—and continue as you were

brushing off the sand, blowing off
the circumstantial him- or her- self

drawn up the ramp of

ASSEMBLY

How could you put forth a plan for
Even as he was uncertain
As pressure mounts on
To give better cause

How could you put forth half
In announcing the spread of
Sound, they from other sources?

EXIT

He fell perfectly. Without property.
He fell immanently. He did not fall. He felt
that: to what does this refer? Please get up

in thresholds to speak with eras—
and haltingly in the units of periphery
pursuant to multiplicities.

VACATE

On one hand
on the other

NOTICE

A small aperture encounters intensities
seizing words and bed
UNDER NEW OWNERSHIP
and bed mussed then unmade
then composed then fabricated then
improved then abducted then
remembered then performed then

Marjorie Welish and Judith Goldman

Interview on "Isle of the Signatories"

November 2008 – January 2009

Judith Goldman: Your poem "Isle of the Signatories" is an unbelievably rich and playful (not to mention incisive, gripping) meditation on (the fallacy of) lyric presence, on the mythic plenitude of the proper name, on "narrative" and meaning in painting, on drafting and creative process, on tradition, intertextuality, and palimpsest, on punning, homophony, and translation, on suspension, equivocation, and ambiguity, on materiality, abstraction, citation, and transmission, on the relation between the "languages" of text and picture—I could go on . . .

In our conversation, I'd like to delve into some of the poem's theoretical concerns and to create/discuss a partial inventory of the poem's intertexts and allusions so as to explore your creative process with regard to these figures.

You've mentioned in a number of interviews and essays that you are interested in a written-writerly-readerly-literary "lyricism" (if I may assert some scare-quotes here—not to signify a verbatim vocative quotation but rather citationality). "What if the lyric were not a voice, were not an utterance but written, hence construed through a presupposition of literature rather than through a presupposition of orality?" is one way you've proposed this alternate lyricality. Zack Finch puts this well in a 2004 review of *Word Group*: "Instead of presenting a voice that reflects on its own nature and what opposes it (as in the Romantic lyric), Welish presents a text that reflects on the nature of textuality and what borders it."

Marjorie Welish: A true sample of the book, "Isles of the Signatories" tries to construct a written voice, a written voice the nature of which is reading and writing. The thesaurus, as Pound would say, is presupposed as a treasury for such a project. If this poem has presupposed a poetics of inscription, it also assumes the responsibility of indeterminacy, or interpretive differentials, that comprise the written system. A poststructural approach to the thesaurus, then, is what is written.

JG: If we might return to your transformation of the Poundian premise of the thesaurus in a bit, I wanted to ask you first about Poussin's painting *Les Bergers d'Arcadie*, a pastoral scene in which a tomb, inscribed with the multiply translatable phrase or motto *Et in arcadia ego*, is surrounding by shepherds engaged in interpreting it . . .

Do you have a long-standing relationship with Poussin's painting? When did you first encounter it / start thinking about it? There are two versions of the painting (1627; 1637); did this have some bearing on your thoughts as you were working on the poem?

Did you have in mind other related art and literature that thematize tombs or the presence of death in the midst of Arcadia (e.g. Virgil's *Eclogues*, Sidney's *Arcadia*, Guercino's *Et in Arcadia ego*, etc.)? I guess I am thinking especially of Ian Hamilton Finlay's public sculptures and prints (such as his print of a camouflaged Third Reich tank in a forest, using the inscription).

MW: As for the specifics, my experience as reader should not distract from the poetics, but, of course, it has informed the poem. The profound indeterminacy of the phrase *Et in Arcadia ego* has seized many imaginations, and continues to replenish itself. Although my first exposure was through Panofsky years ago in college, Ian Hamilton Finlay's political reading only proves the currency of thought that may be read there. The inscription *Et in Arcadia ego* has been historically as well as mythologically tested, and proves itself resilient, because relevant, yet, owing to the interpretive indeterminacy of readings, oracular and, so, perennially true.

With regard to Poussin, much can be said about his studious mentality and that tendency of his to meditate on landscape, attitudes given to revisiting the topic and so to restating it in repetitions that differ, we would say. Yet his 17th-century inquiry may be other than ours. For Poussin, his paintings create prospects that are grounded in classicizing formula as much as they are his expression of that convention, in intimations of observed landscape of a sort that will not be named as such until later, through Constable. In two versions, Poussin's text is a pictural erudition modulating through skeptical queries that render the inscription a speculative feast. That Virgil was already addressing a commonplace, a given of authorship, makes recuperating an original sense of "I" an uncertainty which some would say is a true skeptical enterprise at odds with Panofsky's assumption of the instrumentality of hermeneutic knowledge.

JG: Louis Marin's idea that Poussin's painting "may be characterized as a theoretical caprice" (33), one that deconstructs itself—is it yours as well? Marin's argument about *The Arcadian Shepherds*, laid out in *To Destroy Painting*, notes that, following the classical conventions of history painting, Poussin was generally "translating" a text, knowledge of which was necessary to interpreting the logic of the painting. The viewer is specifically to, "read the painting as the text of a story told by painterly means, but also as the representation of the story's text" (31). (Already here we have a fundamental literariness as referent, rather than an actual scene—though, of course, classical formulae also demanded a familiarity with painterly, not just textual, topoi, in that paintings were to draw on other paintings, not just texts.)

In *The Arcadian Shepherds* in specific, however, Poussin has less created a history painting than a meta-history painting that sets up a parallel between the structure of enunciation germane to a *discursive* narrative history and the structure of representation in a *painted* narrative history (29).

With regard to history as discourse, Marin states that, "A narrative (history) . . . is characterized by a specific mode of enunciation that consists in effacing or excluding all signs of the enunciative process from the resulting utterances: in a narrative (history), the act of enunciation is not itself enunciated. A story [recit], in short, is a discourse without a narrator, a discourse whose narrator is absent" (24). As Marin elaborates, the frieze of figures pointing and gazing in Poussin's image offer "signs of ostension [that] refer to the structure of enunciation" (35). In a way, then, "Poussin . . . seems to occupy the 'metalinguistic' and theoretical position of the linguist who constructs and makes known his basic model of communication" (38). Yet the enunciation at stake, "*Et in Arcadia ego*," is only interpreted and ventriloquized by the open-mouthed shepherd—while it is originally "voiced"—that is, in silence and in writing—by a tomb. Thus, Poussin simultaneously illustrates the denial or suppression of the subject of the enunciation in the act of narration: "In *The Arcadian Shepherds*, it is less a matter of telling a (hi)story than of recounting the representation of (hi)story in its dual relation to writing and death" (26).

The suppression of the narrator in historical discourse—allegorized by the fact that "Ego" is nobody, or a tomb, or writing itself, which produces the subject of discourse who is thus only its effect—is echoed in the disposition of the figures in the painting as well, such that the painting points to a correlative structure of denial of the point of emission of a painting. One sign of the painting's effacement of its own point of enunciation, Marin argues, is its self-sufficiency: it takes neither the painter nor the viewer into its illusion (32).

One correspondence I see between "Isle of the Signatories" and Marin's interpretation of Poussin is the motif of omission in your text, which begins:

> The following lines were omitted.
>
> Even in Arcady I exist.
> e-signature in whose writings
> lies the body
> or its facsimile (3)

[I wonder here whether the lines omitted are in the empty space or whether "Even in Arcady I exist" stands in for that omission, or both.]

Later, on the same page, you write (in an extremely funny passage):

> Attempting to think henceforth
> As a text though ex temporare
> All were reprinted
> With the lyric effect
> His and "there is"
> By adverting to the effect.

And further on:

> To think as the corrected typescript would think
> through the lyric effect
> incited to rhetoric where structure had been.

Followed by an additional line:

I, writing.

You are playing not only with the deferred rhetorical/lyrical effects of writing, but also of mediated forms of writing—the standardized, mass-produced text and the "e-signature." Do you agree with any of this? Or do the motifs of omission and the "thinking text" have other functions here?

MW: Where to begin?! Yes, the speaking voice of the lyric Ego is one already written. Certainly the condition of the voice in the discursive repertory we call "speaking pictures" is of the sort that would animate the meaning of the words' sense (or, in our terms, animate the cultural treasury through use). But not only are cultural truisms already written. The written speaking voice is common enough in literature, and, in this way, "Isles of the Signatories" is making that state of affairs explicit. These matters of literariness I take for granted. Most relevant to my immediate compositional concerns, however, was maintaining the immanent textual register, in writing through a lyric of the written voice.

JG: Another thought about the deconstructive "lyricism" of "Isles": your textualization of voice has a parallel or correlative in Poussin's painting—in that he seems to be textualizing his visual narrative, not by pasting words on a picture (to state the obvious) but more forcefully and fractively by including the textual register within the fictional world of the painting, by means of a motto that, in its office as auto-epitaph, speaks from beyond the grave as can only be done by text (thus pointing to itself as letter) and also thematically enjoining text/Death itself to Arcady, rupturing it. [I'm thinking here of Derrida's premise in "Signature Event Context" in *Limited Inc*: "To be what it is, all writing must, therefore, be capable of functioning in the radical absence of every empirically determined receiver in general. And this absence is not a continuous modification of presence, it is a rupture in presence, the 'death' or the possibility of the 'death' of the receiver inscribed in the structure of the mark" (8).] Poussin himself seems aware of this rupture (or maybe you would disagree?), he's playing on a theme that has already become conventional and thus seems to be indicating the codedness of a message about code-as-text.

Yet (again, yet) it would also seem that by portraying the shepherds in a scenario not just of discovery, but of interpretation, perhaps he is also featuring the problematic of animation, the way the dead letter is always a missed encounter with death (or never altogether dead), since it is instantaneously spiritualized by a reader who enlivens it . . .

MW: Derrida is talking about the iterability of writing—the intention of language to be construed as language and cultural code, whatever it may mean. As already inscribed, the epigrammatic phrase *Et in Arcadia ego* finds itself written into 17th-century or 20th-century art to be read again. That paintings were meant to be read for their teachings until the Impressionists redefined the innocent eye is what makes Poussin's paintings doubly inscribed. Literary theory of a post-structuralist sort complicates the reading of such visual works, however, by interrogating the registers of written and read functions in art, and such theory finds didactic art of the 18th century especially amenable. This is where Louis Marin joins the post-1968 revolt against structuralist and other formalist art criticism. (Note, however, that Yve-Alain Bois does not; staying the course, he, in *Painting as Model*, resists the "French-afflicted" literary belletrist approach to art criticism but continues the project of formalism by other means: through a reading of the plastic sign, not the iconic sign.)

Commemorative inscriptions lend themselves to the expanded field of textual studies, if only for capturing a condition perpetually tantalizing, wherein writing and reading remain problematic. Authorship, readership, literature—all have become the property of a literary theory that takes liberties with art historical discourse.

Marin's narratological analysis of Poussin's later version of the theme—why does Marin ignore the fact of the first?—tests how a history painting (as he calls it) reads under the auspice of the semiotic framework. (Actually, Marin does not entirely ignore the earlier version but dwells on the later version because it demonstrates a structurally configured scheme of reading messages being transmitted.) The historical painting informed through Neo-Classical aesthetic theory takes its mandate to represent as a unity of time and co-present space, Marin maintains, the diachronic cast on the synchronic screen that is also the painting itself. This can be done, Marin writes, thanks to LeBrun's mandate to depict the telling moment or crux of a story that is usually about an ethical dilemma (I am thinking of David's *Oath of the Horatii*) or recognition scene (Greuze), but not always so dramatic: as Diderot's coverage of the 18th-century Salons indicates. It is no wonder that post-structuralist and post-modernist literary theorists alike find case studies for their work in the premodernist art.

So, were that to be translated in a poem of a modernist sort, the continuous present tense having been attained through Mallarmé's compositional musicality and spatialization, an inscription *Et in Arcadia ego* sustains a reading that suspends historical and mythic pasts in thought. Meanwhile, as you say, a metahistory makes evident the discursive character of such a represented thought: discursive critical readings that continue to accrue, Panofsky's and Marin's included. What is the poem in relation to all this? An answer might be that it is a reading that presupposes a perspectivism of frameworks, say, hermeneutic and semiological, as plausible through an imaginative construct of a critical poetics, that the poetics of difference constitutes the object. (A poem or painting is not a thing; despite all projections onto it as a commodifed thing for those who cannot read the cultural nexus. The art object is a set of cultural functions yet also the locus of interpretive engagements in time, and this perhaps is the reason that semiotics of text finds familiar ground in legal studies that acknowledge legal precedent as culturally specified and historically negotiated.) Beyond the incommensurablity of interpretive frameworks that constitute a poetic object pointed at, another answer, more directly related to your question, might be that if for the Neo-classical narrative the chiasmus of "reading—enunciation" marks the crucial ethical moment, then what does the post-structuralist find here but a rhetoric of such a logic. A rhetoric and an indeterminacy of differentials for the inscription, the inscription that would impart its wisdom.

JG: Could you say, in regard to this, a bit more about how this book/poem takes "a post-structuralist approach to the thesaurus"?

MW: Perhaps we read the thesaurus—Pound's term—for the treasury that is culture and our cultural capital.

JG: And about how the epigram *Et in Arcadia ego* has been "historically as well as mythologically tested"?

MW: A framework not discussed by Marin is literacy. The advent of modernity begins with written—as it distinguishes itself from oral—culture, and this re-ignites interest for the post-structuralist who would contest the primacy of speech. Getting back to Poussin's later version of the inscription, note that the shepherd's finger points beyond the penumbra of his shadow cast and so beyond the image inscribed on the wall, to the written precept. A salient socio-linguistic reading of this gesture would note the orality of culture for shepherds (as for most everyone in Arcady), and would maintain that the representation of this situation warrants the shepherd's appeals to the mythic mediator inserted "there" for interpretation.

"Isle of the Signatories" tries to construct a zone for the written enunciation, certainly. Included here would be the documentation of documentary speech acts, such as testaments, as well transcripts of enacted testimony, yet also the archive of this in modern literature. My poem "Epitaph" incorporates Pound's citing of Villon's citing his illiterate mother, for another instance of enunciation, i.e. the re-presentation of writing—through translation, no less—the perfect problematic for displaced difference. Although Poussin encrypted meanings and so provided the opportunity for the hermeneutic interpretation of the painting, Panofsky actually orders his essay as a intellectual history of ideas and does not superimpose a hierarchy on the historically accumulated interpretations of the oracular phrase—up to and including Flaubert's incomprehension of it. My interest in textual strategies leads me elsewhere.

JG: Along these lines, in "Isle" you seem to be staging, rather frontally, a confrontation between voice and letter or text—while you may also be set on undermining the self-presence of voice as such, both literally and figuratively textualizing it, especially by referring to the voice of Marni Nixon, "The Voice of Hollywood" who dubbed the singing of Natalie Wood in *West Side Story*, Audrey Hepburn in *My Fair Lady*, and Deborah Kerr in *The King and I*. As Section 8 of the poem reads:

> I, too, am in Arcady
>
> (signed) Marni Nixon
>
> the unpaginated voice (7)

For one thing, this mention indirectly points to a disjunction in the medium of film, between its sonic and visual components; likewise, to a disjunction in fictive character, who relies on differing voice- and body-props to realize and sustain itself within the diegesis. Here, too, is the idea that a voice has "signed" itself, is a "signature," to which pertains (*pace* Derrida) the structure of iteration and non-self-identity (which in turn spoils the propriety of the proper name, as it becomes signifier (and code)).

Yet, at the same time, in these lines at least, that the voice is "unpaginated" hints that it sometimes escapes the structure of text—that regardless of her ventriloquism of so many characters, Nixon has a voice that bears its own inimitable grain, is the locus of a singular embodiment . . . (Marni Nixon and/or her voice are modified as "unpaginated" three times in the poem.)

MW: Nice way to put it: "staging, rather frontally, the confrontation" between voice and word. What about this? The sign of the voice is reallocated (as Godard, Fassbinder, Wenders, Syberberg—certainly as Brecht does) by constructing literariness. Acknowledging the artifice and making the sign of the voice conspicuous establish the directness you suggest. Scoring for voice does not go unquestioned with the above auteurs of theater and film; neither does it go unquestioned in jazz, where the resources of vocalese, not to mention skat, continue to teach poets who choose not to write concrete poetry. Modern composers such as Berio and Ligeti, not to mention the electronic composers, have made a point of the voice as sign by rendering expressivity as conventional code or by exaggerating the signifiers of such expression. The materials of the voice or the voice as written or voice as designated through literary theory can be pushed into the foreground or assigned unaccustomed positions. Voice-over and ventriloquism are merely obvious post-modern instrumentalities for enhancing the already written register of the spoken word.

As for the unsung (!) role by Marni Nixon's vocals, a peculiar division of labor takes place for "I": authorship is composite, with the auditory and the visual compiled from different persons here unequally credited with creative presence. Indeed, the actor gets the credit for singing, but the singer does not get credit for performance.

JG: Do you see a continuity between this poem/book with other of your interrogations of lyricality—or does it represent more of a departure?

MW: *Isles of the Signatories* demonstrates an ever more concerted attempt to create a lyric poetry from critical and theoretical instrumentalities put in place early on, as early as some of *Handwritten*, although each successive book is ever more explicit in its tactics. Certain approaches, like deploying revision to construct the absence of originary texts and to suspend or delay thought processes, have been in place from the start, however. Difference and differentials within repetition constitute the themes yet also the procedures from the outset, only these commingle with diverse subjects in earlier poetry of mine. With each book the textual strategies announce themselves as object more clearly, more consistently.

JG: In an interview with Matthew Cooperman, "Diagramming Here," you suggest that the speculative element of your work involves "rhetoric": "My poems investigate and organize words and sentences as such, yet also the rhetoric posed through propositions in asserting, denying, and questioning in conventions we have learned to call discourse . . . poetry I write brings attention to the speculative gamut."

In conversation with Bob Perelman, for the conference on your work, you define the process of "rumination or speculation" that occurs in your work as a kind of recursive revisiting of initially posited frames in order to get at the "probabilities of poetry."

Do you see the form of speculation you are engaged in in "Isles" as akin to these rhetorical and iterative investigations?

MW: Several kinds of speculative activities are involved. Repetition can be an instrumentality for germinating thoughtfulness, if only through a process of permutation, which does not measure but changes the textual substance of the poem. Revision lends itself to this process and outcome. As does note-taking of all sorts. As does the performative return through teaching. The grammar of thoughtfulness is one thing, but the grammar of theoretical speculation may be another, at least it is to me, in allowing not only the drift but the algorithm, not only the free association but the array or a serial progression or a spectrum, to construct a theoretical framework—rational orders taken as modes of thought in themselves. Critical thought may merge theory and criticism, but enhancing their difference is another source of speculative activity. Although poststructuralism demonstrates the rhetorical standing of logic, constructing potential poetry through textual strategies induces speculation on a theoretical plane.

Rhetorical and iterative investigations become more and more pronounced in my work. The sequence "Thing Receiving Road" in *The Annotated "Here"* speculates on Stevens's choice of the word "place" rather than "found" in "Anecdote of a Jar," but is not itself a set of landscapes; rather a consideration of Stevensian phenomenological diction provokes the critical experiment I conceive in response. If by "speculative" we advance a theory of the imagination in the name of an ultimate reality, mature and late Stevens would qualify; his earlier works are more various. As for my response to his poem, neither the formal games conceived in advance for the set, nor the iterations dedicated to writing as a discourse are speculative in this sense, and do not concern themselves with ultimate reality, but, rather, through serious linguistic play they realize the potential of poetic discourse. In what sense can procedural poetics realize a reality? "The Logics" from *Word Group* constructs a passage from rudimentary to sophisticated sentences informed of pragmatic questions, demands, and descriptions. Similarly, for the prose poem "Fibulae Iterated," found in *Isle of the Signatories*, several types of functional themes find expression in the pragmatics of questions, reductive narrative statements, and instructions—not sequenced but distributed throughout an operational field.

JG: Could you talk about the relationship between "Isle of the Signatories" and "Art & Language Writes an Epitaph"? Both poems are preoccupied with monumentality / encryption-inscription (or monumentality as encryption-inscription, the latter manifesting this in part through its sections in all caps). But the latter work also takes up the problem of marking the when of "modernity," a ground "zero" that is also a fold in history, a fold that gives rise to derision/laughter through a structure of

1. A knowing, parodic citationality of the past;
2. A radical split from the past that forecloses decisive interpretation (laughter a subjective effect/affect of this asymptotic relation, the impossibility of knowing, which we can also turn into a form of mastery);
3. The continual question of whether modernity is over, or whether it's even begun, coming to a *reductio ad absurdum* in the seriality of the interment of pasts (temporality of "eternity") the poem alludes to.

Do you see this poem as a commentary on or continuation of "Isle"?

MW: Good question. Although not directly responding to a specific poem, it is a commentary, if a deliberately plotted textual strategy can make us mindful of the expressive register. In three parts, "Art & Language Writes an Epitaph" is speculative in the sense usually meant, that is, occurring in the genuine question "When did modernity begin?" Posed as ontology, addressed to ultimate origins, the question is impossible to answer for certain, although answers are forthcoming. From a world perspective, modernity is said to begin with secularization; alternatively, it is said that from a European perspective modernity appears in progressive ideologies. Posed as epistemology, answers may issue in skeptical knowledge or in relative knowledge historically framed, such as: modernity begins with the invention of zero. In the first part, plausible answers as well as wild guesses are forthcoming, and accumulate as the problematic is addressed. With each iteration of the question another answer is added both revising and undoing the prior answer: a consequence is sedimentary rather than logical knowledge.

Perhaps that is too complicated. So, to simplify: throughout the book *Isle of the Signatories*, inscription is never very far from my mind, and is under direct consideration in "Art & Language Writes an Epitaph." The first part constructs modern inscription in paratactic lines, each of which is functionally distinct and pragmatic; the functions repeat throughout the first part, conducted line by line, with phrased metaphoric and metonymic registers and with imperatives and questions, distributed equally throughout the stanzas. The second part asks "When did modernity begin?"—a question which, phrased as an ontology, cannot be answered except insofar as origins become posited genealogical hypotheses. The third part gives scenographic passage to modern figural language from a postmodern vantage—I was actually thinking of Syberberg's nature morte with which opens his *Parsifal*. All performed iterations concern modernity from a post-structural or post-modern perspective—or so this author says.

How does Art & Language relate to this? As a Conceptual collaborative comprised of artist/critics from the U.K. working as a post-formalist research group from 1971 on, it has asked certain questions: What is modern art? And has answered them—in praxis. It performs critiques, sometimes by reenacting art practices and querying them for underlying assumptions, or for unarticulated social protocols. My poem "Art & Language Writes an Epitaph" performs these language experiments concerning modernity's inscription. Post-structural differentials and post-modern historicism included.

JG: Could you say a bit about the two recent artist book projects you have done with Granary Books? I utterly love the play with symmetry and the literalization of the fold in your work with Buzz Spector, *The Napkin and Its Double*—did you see a connection here between this book and your project in *Isles*? Or was there something you wanted to say about the relation between the visual and the verbal as germane to this project in particular?

MW: At the initiative of Granary books, two collaborative projects in art and writing have come about. When I spoke of my admiration for the work of Buzz Spector, Steve Clay showed me a cafeteria napkin on which Buzz had drawn a proposal months before. This then became the first step of our collaboration. Imagine this: his sketch, handed over to me, becomes the original for a copy, done by duplicating each phase of its unfolding onto glassine folded in imitation of the napkin, now with a verbal element pasted inside. Buzz (who hadn't known of my intervention) then names the result. Constructing the proposal for a book rather than the book as such imports drawing into writing; working the napkin's double by unfolding it brings writing into drawing but does not return it to its original state. The semiotics of "The Napkin and Its Double" is indeed complex.

Another project initiated by Steve Clay became an undertaking two and a half years in the making, *Oaths? Questions?* was published early in 2009. For this I invited James Siena to be my visual and verbal interlocutor because both of us, each in our own way, think with rules and operations generative of worlds. The book is built of images and writing done by both myself and James Siena—the conception from the outset as I had envisioned it was the distribution of writing/painting and reading/seeing across pages, for which purpose opaque paper would be interleaved with transparent pages (mylar), allowing superposition of text and image such that as turning pages demonstrates the text, legible as writing but not intelligible for sense, it becomes both legible and intelligible (yet not entirely disclosed). Our shared tactical approach, not the specific decisions, makes our shared project coherent from the start even though as the project evolved we consulted each other relatively infrequently and pursued our own ways of doing things. Initially, I did theorize the relation of words to image and construct a distribution of writing/painting and reading/seeing back and forth across the pages, left to right and right to left. Ultimately, what I'd envisioned was realized. Fortunately!

JG: What seems important about *Oaths? Questions?* is not only that its elements—text and image—work together, but also that the material construction of the book imposes limits, as you put it, on the "distribution of writing/painting and reading/seeing"—its particular material format is essential to it. As you note, when text is superimposed on image, it is legible as writing (or print), but not yet entirely sensical (because not yet wholly intelligible as determinate language, as on pages where the color of the painting blacks out portions of the text or where lines in the painting/drawing seem to cross out or cancel the text). As the pages of the book are turned, text is lifted off image and thus becomes legible and intelligible, but is still nonetheless, as you state, "not entirely disclosed." What impedes this disclosure, as you see it? Is it that there is no way for the reader to apprehend this text in a plenitude of meaning or state of completion, since by seeing it with the image, one can't really read it, while seeing it alone deprives it of its context within the work?

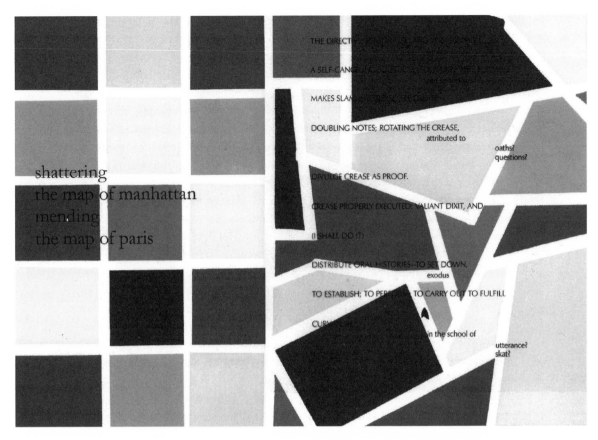

THE DIRECT...

A SELF-CANCE...

MAKES SLAN...

DOUBLING NOTES; ROTATING THE CREASE,
          attributed to
                                        oaths?
                                        questions?

DIVULGE CREASE AS PROOF.

CREASE PROPERLY EXECUTED: VALIANT DIXIT, AND,

(I SHALL DO IT)

DISTRIBUTE ORAL HISTORIES--TO SET DOWN,
          exodus
TO ESTABLISH; TO PER... TO CARRY OUT TO FULFILL

CURV...
                          in the school of
                                        utterance?
                                        skat?

shattering
the map of manhattan
mending
the map of paris

from *Oaths? Questions?* by Marjorie Welish with James Siena

In your artist's note on the Granary website, you put this slightly differently, stating that with the superimposition of text and image, what the reader first encounters is "the obstructed construct of art seen through a verbal screen." I am interested here in two things: 1. That per your description the "art" below or through the text is already (merely?) a construct, which is obstructed by what we might more usually understand as a construct, the language that inevitably—and here literally—imposes an interpretation on what we see. 2. That while, as you note, by turning the page the reader shifts to reading "language excavated or broadcast from the surrounds," you seem less concerned with the state of the image now denuded of text. How exactly do you see the reformatting of your painting in the book as "deform[ing] its own grid"? And further, as the text now stands on its "own" as poem, does its being broadcast from the surrounds of art—from or past its margins—deconstruct the original sense we get of the verbal obstructing the visual? Are you showing (contrary to what I suggest above) that excavation of layers is possible?

MW: In the most general sense you're inquiring about the poetics of the book, the illuminated or illustrated book in particular. As I have said, first came the decision to distribute word and image by interleaving transparent and opaque pages—all to create an interference of the word's graphical, formal, and cognitive aspects, even as the image is impinged upon and also changed in the process. How one interprets this depends on one's theory of modern literature: difficulty, deemed a positive value in the modernist scheme of things and in poetics as different as the Symbolist Mallarmé, the Vorticist Pound, and the Objectivist Zukofsky. To read for text, then, is to acknowledge difficulty as providing the potentiality for not being able to see, not being able to read, as well as being able to see but not read, read but not see, and to see and to read. For instance, once I determined that my images would derive from a certain painting from 1983–4 built of juxtaposing predetermined with intuited grids, I created several works without referring to the original because the conceptual envelope of given and improvised ordering was in mind and remained my salient point of departure. So while working off this idea —the conceptual envelope—I went on without yet knowing the particulars. To return to the interference—productive interference—between reading/seeing and understanding, I should mention that the original painting has made an appearance in the constructed book. By inserting a slide of the painting in its own page, an image identified as an image whether or not it is decipherable in its particulars, we make seeing something other than self-evident. Distancing effects in the creative manipulation of my formal logics were productive in engendering dissociated, occluded, and yet also coincident—what?—events. The experience of reading and seeing distributes differently for the reader than for the author, the one who writes and paints.

Meanwhile, I had begun the verbal compositions before I settled on the visual work. These poems, composed from a given lexicon (table/tablet/entablature; sign/signature; crease) were not written to specific images, although slight adjustments occurred later in the compilation of the pages.

JG: James Siena gives a beautiful gloss on the book's title in his statement on the Granary site: "And the words offer hints to the truth (oaths) and doubts about them as well (questions). Their very transparency evidences the debt they owe to the wordless visual." Do you agree with this latter point? In a sense, you seem to be saying that it is in their state of superimposition that the text seems transparent, while lifting the words off the opaque page so that they stand on mylar alone materializes them . . .

MW: But the book's construction tests the sign of reading: material transparency is not to be taken for transparency of sense. James Siena's phase "wordless image" may be his way expressing a poetic truth of visual versus verbal arts conventionally. He certainly had been invited to explore the possibilities of image-making on his own terms. Although he delighted in the initial set of opaque/transparent conditions lent to painting/writing and seeing/reading, he adapted these to his style and, assuming his own practice as the point of departure, created labyrinthine drawings developable from a deceptively simple procedural rule. James continued to do just that, but what interested him was to develop the labyrinth or maze-like form by augmenting the drawing in palpably incremental color-coded stages, each of which was to remain visibly distinct and in sequence. He was so engaged in a spatial display of the temporality of his image method. Moreover, to his real credit he did not stick to his own preset path but

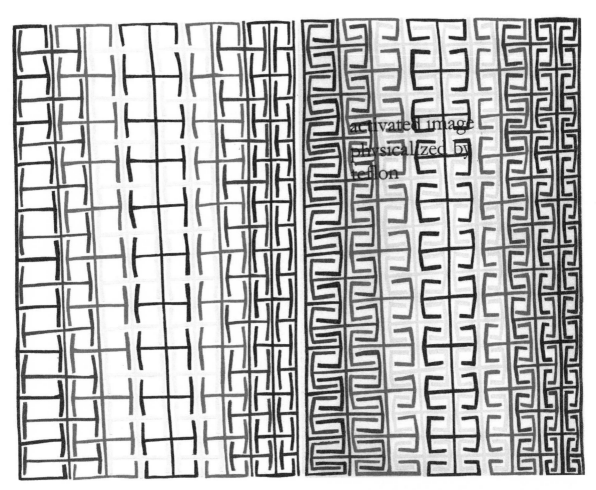

activated image
physicalized by
teflon

from *Oaths? Questions?* by James Siena

scrupled to revise and even cast aside image ideas until he was satisfied with the relation of the image to the page and book. James further accepted the challenge of writing words to his own images and my own—he becoming a respondent, as I had become a respondent to his images. Note that we do not identify who is doing what, except through style. Our authorship is not secret; it is in the work.

JG: Could you say a bit more about your description of both Siena and yourself as artists who "think with rules and operations generative of worlds"—worlds that are not, as you explain "ultimate realities," but rather operational fields or fields of poetic discourse whose various (even inexhaustible) potentialities you draw out through "serious linguistic play"?

MW: As the Granary Books website indicates, we largely worked independently and could do so given the similarly tactical thought that informs our creative work. Although not so radical as the independence of like minds informing Cunningham/

Cage collaborations, *Oaths? Questions?* does presuppose that precedent. When James speaks to the distinction between the word and the wordless as though to assume a classical distinction between the modes of mark-making constituting verbal and visual work, I acknowledge the framework for which this is a statement, despite the fact that for post-structuralists the mark is the *arche*-writing through which the modes of writing and speech—or, for that matter, writing and drawing—split off. (Blake would conjoin them in his calligraphic books where writing and drawing integrate; indeed, Blake's poetic ideology insists on the truth of unified drawn and written modes.) Under debate is whether the visual and verbal can ever be utterly distinct. Although not in favor now, the structural distinctiveness implied in James' statement is not irrelevant. Certainly it is not irrelevant to the formalism that informs his artistic practice. Moreover, formalism is not to be discarded as merely aesthetic, as for instance the formalism of some mathematics proves. The poetics of maths and logics generative of poetic fictions still has something to teach us: a way of organizing the experiment that is potential poetry. Algorithmic moves link James' art with procedural poetics of an Oulipean sort. Coincidently, my long-standing interest of pairing incommensurate orders, rational and intuitive, relates to Raymond Queneau's Oulipean concatenation of rational and empirical thought.

JG: Could you further connect this kind of speculative or indeterminate procedural poetic process to your concern for materialist history, as in your critique of Marin's failure to mention the fundamental orality of the shepherds Poussin depicts? In other words, you push beyond formal iteration of possibility because your composition process is recursive, always radically resituating or reframing the elements you began with—but also because you have a concern for the historical context (or maybe better put, the speech-act context) within which the poetic discourse you isolate and work with is activated.

Further, there are so many references to pleats, folds, and warps in *Isles* . . . how does this figurative invocation of iteration or iterability (among other things) relate to speech-act (one way of thinking materialist context) as you see it? (This query seems related to the content of *Oaths? Questions?* as well, in that at least some of its text comprises a preoccupation with speech act and/as event, as well as the figure of the crease: "SIGN ACROSS THE DEICTIC"; "TO ESTABLISH; TO PERFORM, TO CARRY OUT TO FULFILL"; "utterance?/skat?"; "HAVING LEGAL FORCE IF INITIALED, IF CREASED/expel" . . .)

MW: The inscription being pointed to on the tomb [in Poussin's painting] compiles modes of the mark or of mark-making, including the shadow, epigraphic lettering— and to the delight of post-structuralists—the split in the tomb represented. Although Derrida might say "cleft," why not say: A crease? A crease that has escaped notice? Interfered with legibility? A feast for interpretive activity, the sign that is the inscription in all its avatars, including misfires in communication, is being pointed to, and can convey the message: "What's this?" Suspended here is the question, presumably oral, in the inscription that is in the painting. Put another way, within the fiction that is the painting, performative acts of asking (in effect: "Could you tell me the meaning of this?") conflate saying and doing. (In the didactic painting which has a long tradition of dis-playing the sign: to show different signifying aspects of authorial intention and different signifying aspects of reading that intention, through the assembly of figures' performing affect or gesture.) Literary theory and speech-act theory are often in conflict about fictional discourses and the speech acts invoked. The poet-grammarian Emmanuel Hocquard has been devoted to finding a poetics for just this problematic. In a sense, however, as fascinating as this may be, the Poussin painting plays a more important role in our discussion now than it did in my concerns with "Isle of the Signatories," for which inscription of writing and speech as writing, rather than a dedicated rendering of a particular inscription, was the pursuit.

For several years prior to writing poems that became a book, I had been reading and thinking about the issue of inscription in the following way: whenever we, collectively, are called upon to write a commemorative inscription, we tend to revert to classicizing or romanticizing poetics; what would a (post)modern inscription look like? It is this question that informed *Isle of the Signatories*, the book largely written at Cambridge University on a fellowship, but I am still thinking about the issue in these terms. While there I finished a commissioned chapbook for which I selected and verbally framed inscriptions that proved to be a testing ground for what follows.

JG: Could you say a bit more about the commissioned chapbook on inscriptions?

MW: Publisher Stuart Mills sponsored "Poets Poems," a series of pamphlets distributed mainly through a network of poets in the U.K., a series that ran to twenty-one numbers before ending in 2006. Poets became guest-editors, each poet chosen complied by selecting about a dozen poems to be put in chronological order and published without comment. I both complied and violated the rule of no commentary. My own initiative was poems that lent themselves to being read as inscription, starting with the (to us) anonymously authored "The Silver Swan," to which Orlando Gibbons wrote music, and ending with Harryette Mullen's "Why You and I"; the appendix listed for each of my choices comprises key terms framing contextual significance. For instance, appended to "The Silver Swan" is:

> Frame: elegy
> Frame: epigram
> Frame: English madrigal
> Frame: secular vocal music
> Frame: authorship

while listed for "Why You and I" is:

> Frame: abecedecary
> Frame: substitution
> Frame: OuLiPo
> Frame: signfyin(g)

As for *Oaths? Questions?*, the project that follows *Isle of the Signatories*, inscription is still the issue, with poetry derived in part from the adjudicating claims for damages in legal discourse yet also from transcribed speech in modern poetry, from the *Cantos* to jazz lyrics.

JG: It's important that you bring up the difference between "inscription of writing and speech as writing" and "a dedicated rendering of a particular inscription." Epigraphy is a study of particular inscriptions—whereas you are engaged in a kind of meta-epigraphy: a study of the post-modern contexts and fields of expectation and possibility for public inscription tout court. One way this interrogation could link the inscription of writing and speech as writing is through the status of public inscription in a digital culture, in which differentials between speech and writing [to my mind] have in many ways collapsed . . . Perhaps the remainders/revenants of such differentials are what you are mining in *Oaths? Questions?* as you thread modern[ist] poetry's transcribed speech through legal discourse?

MW: You are right. If modern ordering involves analytic thought that gives pride of place to structure, what happens in legal discourse is that structure readily translates to function; and its narrative is the working out of functional relations as much as anything. So, with the language of contracts and contractual relations through semiotic and other approaches in mind, I created poems of the verbal possibilities, some of which may be read in that work (*Oaths? Questions?*). Contractual intention and volition being reciprocated in the signing of one's name, with agreements valid or invalid under certain conditions—especially regarding whether or not a signature appears or where it is placed on the document: on the same surface as the contractual text, on the outside surface. In effect also are deictic relations between "I"/"you" and "we"/"they"; "today"(dated specifically)/"tomorrow" is specified. Conventional as it is, the law can be proposed as a semiotic square comprised of duty and power and a model be built of functional relations between "obliged" and "not-obliged," "authorized" to do and "not authorized" to do. Adjudicating matters for specific situations, legal ambiguities, and disputed semantic territory comprises the interpretation and its domain of indeterminacy. There is poetic potential in this. Yes, in a way the poem's permutational tolerance for verbal play is productive of those remainders unattended to. Non-sense has its uses. Again, as we mentioned, tactics for generating interference patterns between the rational and the empirical scheme of things provides a framework for the Real in post-analytic terms.

JG: The poem "Epitaphs" plays even more explicitly with epigraphy than the poem "Isles" does—and it also uses a technique involving a kind of recursive fanning out from an epitaphic (or perhaps faux-epitaphic) phrase, in this case, *"Pouvrette et ancienne,"* as you say, a phrase Pound cites on behalf of Villon's illiterate mother. (This is so interesting—certainly points back to the shepherds, no?) Is there a link you want to establish between your poetics of recursivity (versus repetition!) and epigraphy/inscription? How do you see recursivity and inscription working differently/similarly in these two poems?

MW: Epigraphy in a traditional sense was certainly on my mind when I wrote "Epitaph" and the differences between epigraphy and inscription. (By the way, here is an instance of what I mean by a crease or fold, with temporal situations implicated in categories of literacy):

Littering.   Litter gravitates toward the spaced

    Creases   the imbricated spacing yet it distributes differently

        Think of epochs and historical formations

    Of courtyards: everything in its place   may be an oath
           A quarter turn?

        Unlettered   a new archive

        I know   I don't other

In *Isle of the Signatories*, all the poems gathering repetitions through iteration do so in the writing process of returning, revisiting, and revising the same materials. I've relied on a recursive creative process since my first book: yet here repetition becomes the explicit topic and domain of inquiry. Aside from "Fibulae Iterated," which distributes differently worded but functionally repeating requests, instructions, et cetera throughout—that is, before performing an operation on the sense, other poems in the book rewrite given materials but so that words repeat but sense phases in and out of possible worlds—here, I'm thinking of "Of Henceforth (Instrumental Version)"; elsewhere, a patchwork of maxims and facts concerned to represent "No" and "Zero" construct a loose federation of lyrics. "Unfolding Yes" is the poem, a poem in parts and in contraries.

So recursive process is enlisted from the outset to be productive of sense, and, yes, productive of repetition—in its kinds and degrees of difference.

JG: And do you feel in *Isles* or in *Oaths?* that you've come to any sense of what postmodern inscription should consist in?

MW: Postmodernism, of which kind? Knowledge, a project and projection of modernity, is an object of a sort. Not a thing as such so much as an organization of cultural categories according to a narrative or a plan, the object of knowledge some would call postmodern, under renovation in reference books and course texts, organizes material through networks of functions and categories with values other than those considered self-evident. In this experiment, educators test discursive habits. Some poetic objects of interest come about in consequence of this with regard to writing and reading.

Judith Goldman

But to me [redo]   Ad terminem

[yawns] I've been bulling a doozy of a doze

Ready to Give the world
                    a big warm hug

    You don't know your own strength

Some beating and calling out at distant doors

    Sign for the parcel

It's my blanky

Blankly

front and back of language

How you were called into the picture

In broad daylight but in a narrow frame

figure cropped by left border

Caught in desire

will this index expiate?

What grudge against me?

    We didn't know you didn't know

At times it is difficult not to lose one's patience

Standing in the gap where it should take place

Perpetual retraction from the expanse,

Open sourced hovel of the world

Come in out of the rain
Wipe your feet

Whereas this fiction finds no quarter, not even

A brutal snagging

Before folding back to its original prospect

the bone dropped me
from its mouth

Into the river
to Catch my image

As if it had been conceived as an illustration for a text

But that suggests my disappearance

The frame is an equal partner in the work

It cannot be torn open into an outside and an inside

No sooner done than said

At least, that's not the picture I get

If only because I can open the door again

> *You're paying for another day because you exceeded the discharge time*

Fine

SO ON THE LAST DAY of this particular narrative

Language forestalls objections to its jurisdiction

But They mean beyond themselves, they live beyond their meaning

Here a single grape seems to have rolled away from the bunch

It May be understood as looking backward

So as to register its own place, or prospect, within the narrative

But Please don't take my likeness

The words have had their say

So can you call me by my true name

I'm a john doe
A body of questions and decisions
To sleep perchance
In every letter's little grave

This my facture
Rough or smooth? I switch, I guess
With the sound of its making

I act as though I were in danger of being left behind

But who is there for me to change places with

Such a painting begins to double back
Perpetually constructing its own parameters

Could this be self-erasure?

Dwindling till it shall be no more

      I have been much grieved to hear of the loss you have sustained

A man lost in the woods, doubling on his own track

Was't not to this end that thou began'st to twist?,

Gaze abducted, turned around

Self-inventoried

As things, not words

My sculpture objects to its stone

There are languages that are heavier than others

This dead painting saps conviction

A verbal aspect stressing the completion of the action

My mind is encaustic

The dreamwork does not itself create meaning

Successive backcloths furled up

Shadow thin, we hover in

Unable to speak first

Below the skull, a row of coins has been laid out

Points of reality fatigue

Dashed line indicates the virtual image of the mirror

The eye remains dashed because it is only an image

It is this reciprocal function
When the object turns out to be an image as well?

According to this account, we would need eyes inside our eyes

I myself wear my hat inside my head

To store it up

And so forth

Ah, *this* will make me a fresh skin

Answerable only to itself

> *You said there was nothing could be done*

I have a single thread binding it all

I do not set out from what men say
Nor from men as narrated

I set out from real active men,

Why they can fly no higher, etc.

Silvered the panel above the skyline so that
It would reflect the real sky

A little party loyalty

Financed by

By any stretch of the imagination

By this stretch?

If the dream is predicated on sleep

It will turn back to take the regressive path

You will think I am wandering away

Leaving it to the mercy of

The night's the day's demise denies the moon its . . .

The new day dons its foreshadowing

> *Take off that unforgiving ensemble*

> *No, just put that in the*

> *Stop painting the virgin!*

You'll see on the facing page

that this is a work of glazed ceramic

You'll see on the facing page

a good night's sleep

The frost breaks up and the water runs

While the general sits there

Elbow for pillow

He dreams a more filial inscription

Come in, out of the rain
Wipe your feet

Whereas this fiction finds no quarter, not even

The same word into which the truth disappears

But still I got my share
And with an order not to say who it was from

For it to dissolve into its meaning

Makes its eternities out of

A single perceptual field

My tail streaming behind me

This *is* el dorado, reader

Your face

Paved with gold

Green grows the little fir tree

That

I know not where

Lyn Hejinian

Nothing: A Silent Film

for Gustave Flaubert

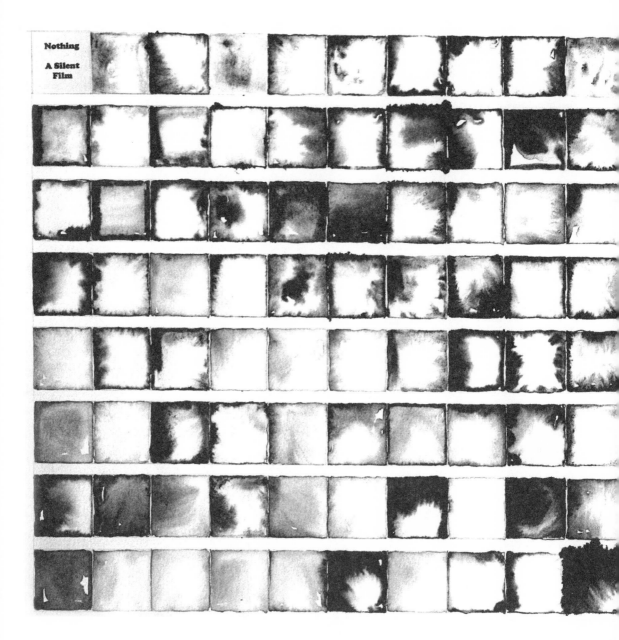

Hejinian notes: "This is a film for Gustave Flaubert who wrote 'I want to write a book about nothing.'"

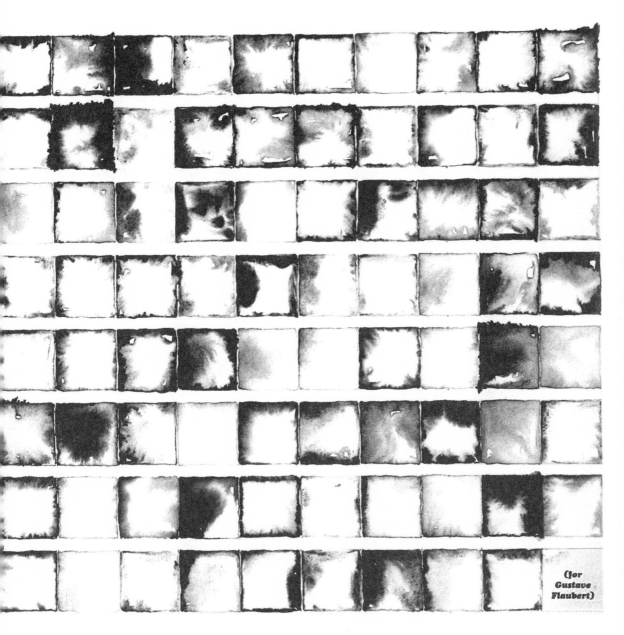

Mei-Mei Berssenbrugge and Leslie Scalapino

Leslie Scalapino asks Mei-Mei Berssenbrugge about Communicating with Plants

Scalapino: One of your recent poems (which you may still be writing), titled "Animal Communication," begins, "I underestimate the power of my connection with other people, with animals and events, / that are coincident." In your poetry, it seems to me that the line and also the poet's and reader's attention are coincident events—formed in relation to (other) coincident events such as thoughts, matter, occurrences. You seem to make, as the text, the sense of a spatial relation to event, that relation (text) being an (other) event itself, as if simultaneous is also consecutive. You mentioned to me that your new poems (of which "Animal Communication" is one) are investigating (or being) a relation to plants. Could we begin by your describing your sense of the new poems making (as having a sense of) relation to plants? As a second part of that question, could you comment on time in/as the poems: is it simultaneous and consecutive at once (as I've cited here), or how would you see that?

Berssenbrugge: First, I want to thank you for having this conversation with me. I find your questions to be profound, beautiful, full of implication and very challenging to answer, because of their richness.

"Animal Voices" uses my research into communicating with animals and with insects. In reality, it is difficult for me to tune into the thoughts of animals or insects. It takes time for me to become quiet and the animals are moving around. I could often receive "instant messages," but what I sent out myself tended to be pressured, and I don't think that is the best way for animals to take in meaning. When I began to read about communicating with plants, I was curious about the "coincidence" that a human illness could be alleviated by a plant, sometimes by a plant from far away, the South American rainforest or a Tibetan plateau. A plant gives me more time to get to know it. I walk every day from the mesa where I live in New Mexico, and I may notice a plant for some reason, because of its beautiful seedpods or the way it shines out with the light behind it. Some people would say the plant is calling to me. Then, I begin to think about this plant, and walk by it, many times. Then, I sit with it. I try to open my heart to it. It takes days of sitting, looking at it, getting to know it. The river bed becomes quiet and vivid. I can hear a bird's wings through the air. Sometimes, I think the whole environment is relating to me through my apache plume bush. I try to feel the embeddedness of all living things with each other, and I try to catch the words passing through my mind, words that are perhaps imagined, but as days pass, I don't think so. I ask the plant to help me with my physical problems. (That seems to be one of the ways plants relate to people.) I read that plants are compassionate, and they are connected by vast mycelial networks underground and by the exquisite receptivity and responsiveness of their chemistries. The same part of my mind that receives word-flashes from animals receives kindly communications from plants. It comes in words without sound in my mind. Do you remember when we were having dinner in New York, and I mentioned to Tom that I read a plant could rearrange its chemistry in order to alleviate a person's ailment? And Tom said, yes, but the question is *when* this happened, and by that I thought he meant that there had been an originary moment, when every element was united. What would make any part whole is intrinsic to all the other elements, and in this case, can be accessed in plants. This brings me to the second part of your question—about the consecution and simultaneity of time and events. Perhaps I am calling on a simultaneity of the originary unity when all connections, illnesses and cures were created, to which I am given access through plants.

To respond to your question about time, yes, I think that time is simultaneous and consecutive at once, and even simultaneous with the future. I have an image that infinite parallel strands comprise one's time (or one's events), past, present and future. Each moment or event projects one line, and you can move from one strand to another, or "pluck" one strand to resonate with the one you occupy or attend to, by your imagination, memory, desire, etc. I think of our sense of passing time or consecution as a perceptual device perhaps like depth perception. An event can also be a measure of time, but there is the sense of event horizon or events triangulating one's sense of space through one's perception and memory. Writing or reading my poem are perhaps extending parallel strands. I hadn't thought of this before, but it's interesting to think of crossing from one strand to another as crossing "space."

Scalapino: Another line in "Animal Communication": "I write down today's encounters, including the mosquito, as a dream to interpret." Could you comment on this fascinating concept: (one's) actual historical event as a dream, and later interpreted—and the relation of that dreaming to past/future (of) (that's) the poem?

Berssenbrugge: Perhaps my subjective assemblage of a day's events or perceptions have a wholeness or coherency or potential depth of meaning that a dream has.

I reject the idea of randomness, that things happen by chance. I see that events make a whole by definition, and that assemblage of experience is assimilated by us. If things are connected, then they can be interpreted in terms of an entity, like a dream. If events happen to you, are your "story," then it can be interpreted, there is resonance. I also see that your intentions and how you see the world affect what happens to you. So, of course, you may interpret your part in it, in creating the assemblage of occurrences and events.

Scalapino: In Section 4 of "Animal Communication," you conceive space as active: "Shade glows with no edge between space, grass. / As shade trees grow and the orchid grows, space around reflects inspirative beauty. / Like time passing of a fountain flowing, passage in space is our perspective opening to / this beauty." In these lines, the passage in space is the person's perspective itself (as such). Is perspective/attention as such, as the space (itself), the poem's relation to 'being' (both action and identity)? That space that's the poem is also 'beings' that are plants and animals? Could you comment on the space that is the poem as a relation to "inspirative beauty," and that beauty in relation to 'being' and 'event'?

Berssenbrugge: You ask about something in the poem that was at the edge of what I could express, and now I'm straining to understand what I wrote. In this section, the camera pulls away to show that speaking to animals is part of a larger picture of expression and its beauties.

I try to grasp time as a perceptual device, a measuring, the way space is also. I thought that the terms of measurement or comparison could vary, such as measuring time by light. Measuring a fountain flowing by time passing, so many gallons per minute, measuring a segment of space by the opening of one's perception to an orchid's beauty.

Rather than time passing or passage in space, I attempt a standard of measure that is spirit opening, and I use the symbol of a fountain. Inspirative is a way of describing the motion of water from the interior of the fountain outward, as we look on it. Your interpretation is wonderful, I could respond that I am trying to express a standard of measure or passage that is our being opening.

If plants and animals, insects, all living things including rocks are an interconnected organism, than we may also be speaking of that being opening, but in "Animal Voices" I was still thinking of one or two people and their perceptions.

Scalapino: I use the word "random" to mean events or phenomena occurring in such a way (appearing as such) that there is no framework or relation that is known yet—or: occurring before its framework is mapped. Perhaps an originary instance is the instant a configuration of relations is perceived as such (is perceived in that way, by one imposing that perspective)? I read many of your poems as being both the instant before there's configuration (perception) simultaneous with the instant of composing some particular relation between the elements. Are you in your texts wrestling with (or the text manifesting) the necessary difference between imposition (imagination, optical illusion, etc) and 'actuality' (whatever that is)? The event occurring as imagination is utterly impermanent without being or/and without being in the sight of others? Do you have the sense of (the intent of) mapping one's (as your) imagination, as say in exchange with plants—which is the same as the actual *enactment* of exchange with plants?

Berssenbrugge: I'm playing with the idea that perception is intrinsic to the originary instance, to creation, if the one perceiving and the instance or origination perceived are interchangeable.

I like your idea of no framework yet, prior to meaning. I would like originary to suggest that the fact that something (a plant) exists means that there was an original frame or instance, which includes myself and the plant. But I may be combining my mysticism with my perception. In my past work I've used the value or magic of perception as a way to make a continuum between separated things, including people.

I don't think about imagination often, so I don't think about its imposition as much as I think about understanding, and I think I may interchange understanding, creativity, and perception. Your work so beautifully uses the act of perception as creative. And it's wonderful when I can feel that in my own writing. I like to think of creativity as a general exterior field outside, not from me. Perception (which is creative) is an access to 'actuality' or at least that is the stance of the poem. The poem itself is the actual actuality, I agree.

So, I don't have a sense of imagination with my plants, at all. My conversations are real, but they are not in a human voice. Words stream through my mind, it's the same kind of feeling as an intuition or when the telephone rings and I know who's calling. And my stance is: this experience is what my plant poems are about, although in reality the poems are assembled from notes from various sources and don't usually describe my experience. The creative assemblage of a poem might be what you describe as imagination's creation of it, that perhaps composing/assembling the poem is the actual. Perhaps for you that is simultaneous with perceptions and events in the world. For me I think the use of "the world," "events," or the actual is an artistic device or conceit for the event of assembling an energy matrix, the poem. I'm still thinking about the simultaneity of all things at the beginning.

Scalapino: What do you mean by magic, what is magic for you?

Berssenbrugge: There's always a gap, and the gap is filled or spanned by what I was going to call magic, but decided on the word, mystical. Then, I forgot to erase the magic in my answer, and you ask about it. Is it magic that imbues value, heart qualities, faith, fairies? The numinousness that instills our sense of value, the numinousness that spans gaps between material investigation and spirit, what Derrida might have meant by aporia. But I think I mean spirit to be a real phenomenon.

Scalapino: Is it possible for you to send a few poems—or at least two or so poems—to print with the interview, which I think will work best with demonstrations as materials of the art?

Berssenbrugge: I think about a concept and write the poems a long time before their final forms, and so here are excerpts from three poems in progress. They are fragments and not as attenuated as my finished work would be.

Mei-Mei Berssenbrugge

FROM Glitter

Thoughts are sent out by one rock informing other rocks as to the nature of its changing environment, the angle of the sun and temperatures cooling as night falls, and even its (loosely called) emotional tone changes, the appearance of a person walking who's not appropriately empathic, because she's lost in her racing thoughts.

Thoughts meet and merge with other thoughts sent out, say, from foliage and other entities.

I tell you that your own thoughts and words can appear to the inhabitants of other systems like stars and planets to us.

Intensities of thought, light and shadow between us, contain memories coiled, one within the other, through which I travel to you, and yet are beautifully undetermined.

For what you say to me is not finished within my thought or memory, but you grow within my memory and change, the way a shadow extends as light passes over it in Akashic emptiness.

You grow through what I have to say to you, as a tree grows up through space, then what I have to say changes.

That's why we need the identity of our physical forms; here, we don't know what's behind physical stars and planets.

FROM Slow Down Now

I've been sitting looking at this plant without feeling time at all, and my breathing is calm.

There are tiny white rosettes, and the whole bush is a glorious cloud of feathery pink seed-heads, here, in the arroyo.

Even with closed eyes, I see flowers in the center of my sight, new flowers opening out with pink petals illuminated by low sun behind me, and small gray green leaves.

There's no stopping this effusion.

Looking at the plant releases my mental boundaries, so time is not needed for experience.

Late afternoon is like a stage, a section of vaster landscape, and my mood is of a summer idyll.

The dry arroyo sparkles around us.

Meaning I come upon on wild land strikes me at first as a general impression,   then joy suffuses me.

I accept that I've aged and that some friends have died.

• • •

One time, you may need a plant you don't yet know, in order to connect pieces in yourself or in a person you are trying to be with.

It may be a rosebush at the end of the road, a summer rose, whitish on the outside of each petal, and pink inside, expressing its gestalt visually.

When a plant receives this kind of communication, it begins altering the wavelengths its chemicals reflect in order to offer itself to your imaginal sight, for you to gather it.

The plant or another person will awake from embedding in the livingness of the world and take notice of your request.

The internal chemistry of plants is one primary language of response that they possess.

Through this method of your perception of its color, its fragrance, an infusion of its petals, you receive not only molecules of plant compound itself, but also the meaning in yourself that the plant was responding to.

So, there is meaning in a chemical compound.

FROM Hello, the Roses

The rose communicates instantly with the woman by sight, collapsing its boundaries, and the woman widens her boundaries.

Her "rate of perception" slows down, because of its complexity.

There is a feeling of touching and being touched, the shadings of color she can sense from touch.

There's an affinity between awareness and blossom.

The rose symbolizes the light of this self affinity.

I come to visit drooping white cabbage roses at dusk.

That corner of the garden glows with a quality of light I might see when light shines through mist or, in early morning, reflects off water.

I stand quietly and allow this quality to permeate the air around me.

Here with a white rose, color is clairsentient, this color in the process of being expressed, like seeing Venus in the day.

E. Tracy Grinnell

Vision(ary) as (re)ordering that's creating our seeing • The Private World of Darkness • *Hell and Lower Evil*

Early this morning, I dreamt I was in the Twilight Zone episode "The Eye of the Beholder" (originally "The Private World of Darkness"), trying to see through the glass and gauze floating in front of my face. In this episode, Miss Janet Tyler (played by Maxine Stuart) is hidden, her face covered with bandages, having undergone multiple surgeries to correct a hideous deformation. This is the final operation, her last chance, and if it fails she will be sent to live in exile in a village with others like her—others deemed hideous by the State. I remember reading at some point that they filmed parts of this episode from Miss Tyler's perspective by placing a camera inside a fish bowl wrapped in gauze. In my dream I was inside the fish bowl, looking out as though from her perspective, my vision obstructed with only the slightest hints of light breaking through the gauze. Of course, this isn't *her* perspective, since she isn't inside the fish bowl, rather, it is the perspective of the camera—recording the experience of blindness, of sight deprivation, and conveying disorientation and anxiety. Waking from the dream, I decided this was an analogy for homophonic translation. And I think now, too, that the dream offers a frame—a vantage point—from which to consider Helen of Troy.

When writing *Hell and Lower Evil*, a homophonic translation of Claude Cahun's *Hélène la rebelle*, I was deliberately *not* performing a (semantic) translation of Cahun's work but using visual and acoustic association to render a new version of the text. The (visual/acoustic) translation happens before *sense* is made in the mind's-eye—an exercise in sens/ory deprivation—so that a new sense is created:

> "Je sais bien qu'il ne me désire même pas"
> "gesture being killed / nemesis desiring my own past"

and in places, departing from the text, set on a path that falls away:

> "Il nous faut, dans les faubourgs de Sparte, une maison de campagne, des enfants, le repos."
> "it no more false / denies the false / bards of Spartan means / decampment, desperate infants / of late repose / / in night / in night / pulse / might rebel its / episodic fugue-logic . . ."

A "hostage of fate" (*Tiger at the Gates*, Jean Giraudoux), Helen of Troy was a devastating vision/ary whose beauty was destruction itself. Maligned for this beauty and as a symbol of the folly of pride and arrogance, of going to war for an illusion, Helen is a projection that doesn't cease to travel—"a name can travel where a body can't" (*Helen,*

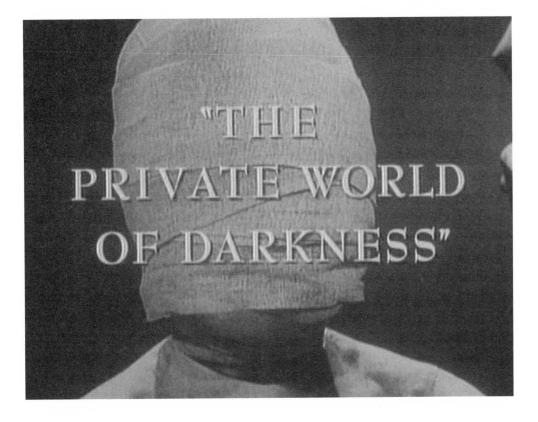

Euripides)—and is therefore prophetic. The voice that emerges out of the non-sense, in *Hell and Lower Evil*, resembles, or re-assembles, Frankenstein-like, *Hélène la rebelle*, and is a recording of *dissociation*, conveying an acute disorientation that nonetheless offers insight. Through blindness and nonsense, new sight and sense. This is a "terribly clairvoyant" Helen, speaking in tongues, revivified and calling out her own projection, which is inherently *other*. Helen has no agency as a "hostage of fate" and therefore can *only* be a projection, never herself. Her vantage point is a vanishing point. We are left holding the projections, so starkly our own.

The twist at the end of "The Eye of the Beholder" is that the surgeries have failed, but when Miss Tyler is unveiled (now played by Donna Douglas), we see that she is in fact beautiful. It is the faces—only shown in shadow and silhouette until this point—of the doctors, nurses, and the State's leader (speaking fanatically on T.V. about conformity) that are deformed, misshapen.

January 25, 2009

vii. cont.

/demagnetization/

assunder
the porticoes
en masse
understudy at competence
severing passes
in meditation

maxims, inscriptions
surely deserved pan-cartes-postales

encroach
the steps
before calculation

~~vvvvveriteeeee-~~

~~eeeeemennnnna-oeillllll-~~!
<scratch that>

(still, very clear night--whether trans-
figured/trans/figure/for a future
still, very, clear)

in night
in night
nearer naught a cant-
alogue)

xi. cont.

comfortable sashay
dangerous chamber
a coterie
it pencils away
all this each game
pending qualified minutes
augmented gradually
indefinitely the numbered
punctual joue
practical system, mastery

jaded possession
the letters
the spirits

jarred for ennui
it is the daring grace
quilled, no sweet

jealously to lesser pretensions
killed, no sweet

killed, no varied

sweet menace!

have reason!

jest we are allayed
by sirens

xii. cont.

nay, by voices
of fascination
serpents of my own regard

I swear being the subtle
Ulysses none recieved
in divine what-others-may-say
in too-little-reproachments

desired compromises
avoidances of my own bays (the moon here
replacments of lakes-cum-seas, reliquaries
for the violence of seaward pathways, marked
and too marked injuries of pathos-cum-
marginalia, what is sing-song darkened
and wanderlusted into soliloquy for this
is my reason,my answer to the sea as it
overtakes...)

so my courted sea
paired it so
lyre-faint too depleasured

so rused oldly, wildly
it is terribly
clairvoyant

gestured being killed
nemesis desiring my own past

xiii. cont.

Alas! Menace!
Exigencies are conquered
killed in operatic
self-same lyres-so-blind

so beatific geese
of artifice and facile
by lovely hours
Ulysses aches of several
monsters, estranged
don't the captors make of the tissue
of your minds-eyes
it fakes the love
of peers such that love's
convenience lies, it delivers
virile dears in parks
so it avails of fallacy
severence

(Paris! your boulevards are like rivers
to mine eye! Your crossings like cinema
your songs like mine...)

it pairs bombastically
killed like a cormorant
could pretend the seriousness
like a road out of Ithaca

xiv. cont.

revived dark
the park so involute
false in survival
in pairs for obedience-sake
and my own cruel epoch

for none procured
a total deuce
let glory immortalize
quail-like,attentive
to the core

quick import
so poor!

inviolesce astray

Helen, she revolts!

Hell never crossed
poor destiny

minus a core
odious to my fill!

I am in reverence
laced to my violent
chest-made satellite

of capriciousness

xv. cont.

shall the travel
stand for you
chagrined, it

without exclamation
in the end
my compensation?

To no longer
play the subtenant
it no more fix false
denies the false
bards of Spartan means
decampment, desperate infants

of late repose

*
in night
in night

pulse

might rebel its
episodic fugue-logic

xxxrain terrain
given like to like
meadow to shadow
in to muse

could careless

Simone Fattal

[Untitled]

The War I know is a brain tumor that sifts every information and sensation that goes through it; and with the years (60 and counting) these paths have thickened in such a way that circulation is chaotic. This War, the worse of it being that it has obliterated all the names, is multiform, and universal. There is not a place in the world where it is not waged, so that these paths in the brain, finally totally obstructed, lead first to speechlessness, then to only one gate, one exit, straight to death.   —*Simone Fattal*

Michael Cross

Pax

> I am reluctant to have this band put on me. But rather than that you question my courage,
> let some one put his hand in my mouth as a pledge that this is done in good faith.
>
> *Snorri Sturluson*

> That sacrifice which has fallen by the right hand of the victor is called the victim:
> when the hostile troops are driven far away then the sacrifice is called the host.
>
> *Ovid*

decas a hand in matte-batting bound in the mouth
worth numerically five, say throat, palate, tongue, worth teeth
not so a lictor rides whips from the skin folds in similar case
swathed hands haven't mass, haven't maw-meats should mouth
exclude sate from the forearm in teeth
pigs fixed by mouth, ham of hand, fingers of foot

cleave as stone drawn straw
oppugn gable ends, ends poist, laid upon a finger
slough off directional stress
shew light, allemande, courante,
light sarabande, gigue, light
light chaconne, transom, kodachrome
the life of my life bound in a bale of life

breathing face measured out in mouthfuls, whelmed whole-head
sacer in a tongue, chin, drape lacquer
issued breath from the end of the leg-bone
and still when the skull's at the bottom of the pile
we lose, mostly, took this one and fastened the share
and coulter to a plough, shaved the tops into honzon
pulled living from the well and fixed our mind on wood

not a single fuck in a pound of chrome alum
in eight, each face lacquered for treasure place
mother fell a well strung a long pole
twigs dipped in blood, a finger-ring my peace
the silex is likely what slit their throats
not the knife, but the stone that made them fall

for "thousand-skull" divide by eight, for eight-face
ends spat in a jar measured in mouthfuls to fashion a man
hewed by first light to fell and fight again
ribcage sprung wings made a ship from it
two-fluids-womb—three-world's-single-heart

dreamt of his blood in the mouth of his brother
like gum-props one jaw for the sky, slavering gape
the lower bone scrapes off ground, salivates
slaughter-gaut, yawned with the arm's mouth
two-youth's white with milk-cured wool
so that laughing there will seem too few when the wolf comes
eight-brow stress the wide island of meadow
bound by the entrails of son

Denise Newman and Gigi Janchang

I've been writing to Gigi Janchang's photos in her series called "Portraits: 2084." Each feature of the face in the portrait is taken from a different source and assembled to create a new face. For example, she's used my six year old daughter's eyes for a portrait of a young man. I became interested in the portraits for what was missing, that invisible glue that integrates the parts. Recently, I finished a manuscript where I'd been thinking through the accident, or one's death, as the vehicle of life (replacing God). These future people seem to be consumed by their accidents, though still alive, as if trapped on the wrong side of it, which is where I want the writing to take place.

Gigi Janchang is originally from Taiwan. She came to the U.S. to study at The San Francisco Art Institute. She's primarily an installation artist. Here's a general statement about her work:

> "Although my eyesight always has been very good, I often play a mind game that I am a blind person who regains vision. This gives me energy—I feel rich with resources. By the methods of composing, emphasizing, or transforming in the process of art making, the work has boiled down to perceptual experiments with objects or mundane environments, for the purpose of making, not so much the objects/environments visible, but the ability to see 'visible.' Via the work, I intend to explore perceptual issues (how we see) and relativity issues (how we think) which are, to me, indeed interesting and fundamental in studying human existence and behavior."

FROM *Future People*

A rational side and another side tempting, within a moral structure, a man lets his pants down across the street from the children, just like the cat who goes out but sits looking in the pane of the door. A moment like that outside but inside, or inside but outside with Larry smoking a cigarette across the street, all day long in dialog, "yeah," with oneself, like buttering both sides of the head and bearing down on a thought hoping to taste a thing of value, "in reality" what gets made is winter—six hollow seeds.

He needs "$19 to go to _____ to fix the fetus" (is that what's said?) softly and the other softens to it—little pussy willow, one wants trust to say "good heart" or "ring of love," she says "fine" like a "distribution mother" all watch her purse—"I can"—"in reality" not in control, the other holds it, this son of a barren man, a "bad Adam" this milk fed milk weed.

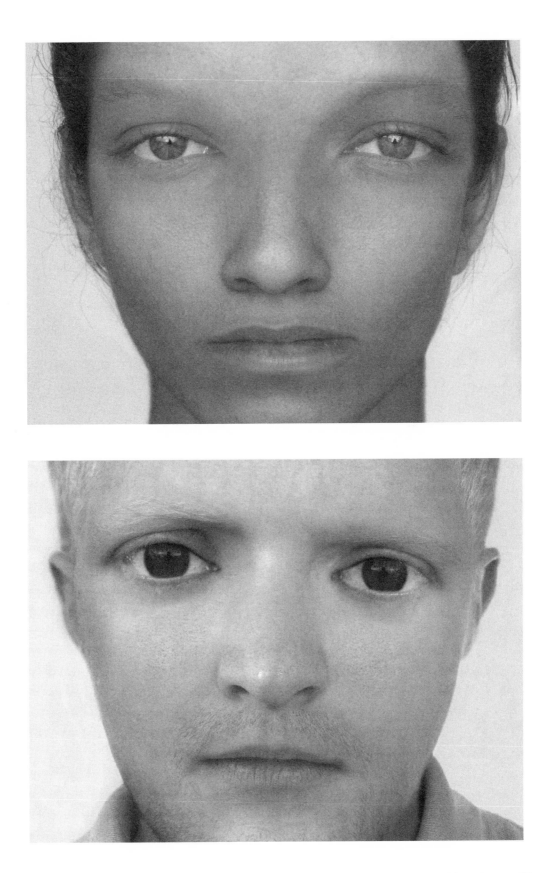

Early-born is attracted to uniform—for further pupating, I guess. The man was very fat and his buttons burst off. Can you sew on fate and fake it? Someone, a public self, coming from the dark end of the hall says "You don't belong in here"—"in reality" it's easy to turn on one's own people—when ordered to, that is. Down the long hall the eye of the badge sterilizes. The other touches there to punctuate, and down they go dizzy down the rocky barrenside of the guard, she thinks "it never ends" and "what happens at the end?" "In reality" the meanest accidents are meaningful.

A girl says "worrier" like "warrior"—"I'm a warrior"—"in reality" they're related, within a moral structure, who gets to determine/be determined, we're all fucked and unknowingly look back towards death each time, can't grasp a thing of the mind, so it has its way with us, the way Saturn ate his children so they wouldn't eat him, "in reality" this is not a mystery. What's missing is a mystery.

Someone's watching her next aisle over bag herself—she receives it in shame—why shame?—"I deserve a brutal ending" thinks, shivers length of arms, continues bagging "in reality" wanted to be a saint—called "show off"—at that time

God watched. Unfathomable brink, down the dark hallway to light and distance—"I can"—come so close to death be alien in life—writing a poem or coming across one in a jar of water—jarring words—"They appear because they are the mind themselves."

Thom Donovan

Eight Poems

I repeat I lose I light I little I logos I ghost I boy I friend I psycho I wound I envy I lens I
prayer I Iraq I perhaps I collapse I harm I no thing I no one I my I invisibles I camera I
Caligula I Indian I admin I eyed I repeat I after I oi I pod I politic I capital I island I fail I
daughter I flower I glow I lame I dumb I lead I silent I become I kill I grasp I thunder I
exploit I invisibles I envy I event I beam I pray I crazy I therefore I whatever I can't I must
I Kant I you I we I state I she I fray I afraid I yes I node I monadic I open I state I no I every
I telling I spelling I kill I heal I on I if I fold I rise I fell I dumb I ethic I ethnic I fantasy I
fancy I judgment I of I four I lack I watch I switch I life I ear I hear I Bush I burn I hear
I kill I like I little I word I mix I encounter I machine I bomb I nation I Prada I border I
parole I poem I hi-fi I flick I cathode I cathartic I soul I law I hugely I dearth I plinth I
mold I explode I bigger I now I make I in I die I mind I ecosystem I system I all I terror I
disaster I feel I withdraw I OK I each I literal I blind I hysterical I moot I dissociate I love
I breach I break I missile I heat I heart I cause I thou I art I earth I unearth I reap I feel I
Sudan I suddenly I weapon I are I weep I expunged I speak I place I seat I aspect I shibbo-
leth I shadow I booby I exit I strategy I weep I tribe I one I parade I lingual I Franco I deep
I silly I man I performance I anxiety I secret I phenomenology I afraid I scab I hiding I
comedy I unseat I prefix I presuppose I empire I revolutionary I tree I dark I empirical I
skin I tag I meet I meek I might I mate I bleed I Jew I Ashura I sure I a I surf I tuck I fire I
revenant I revile I wraith I money I fourth I estate I state I 9/11 I flight I incur I thunder
I Mary I none I note I single I scar I furthermore I mantis I disappear I therapist I magic I
sovereignty I autonomous I pyramid I great I slave I parchment I desert I alphabet I dead
I lost I language I eternal I quaver I below I modulate I voice I cover I conquer I impress I
America I imaginary I stupid I mirror I fashion I furnish I gold I Caesar I burn I bless
I impeach I immune I W I am I continent I sleep I blind I play I bubble I least I crayon I
miscarry I immaculate I just I night I miracle I wind I age I need I necessitate I incite I
plosive I device I decisive I symbol I caesura I shade I Hiroshima I airplane I twin I tower
I Taliban I Japan I invent I fall I give I listen I sing I too I prattle I unknown I barely I
nursery I little I mother I silent I laugh I joy I jab I fast I purchase I prick I will I Nero I
Negritude I Nigger I labor I parole I pig I rife I rifle I struggle I wriggle I mind I mingle
I refuse I solve I dissolve I fall I grow intense I stress I body I theme I Marker I Rainer I
Biafra I depict I portrait I dream I sunlight I midnight I aleph I anarchy I early I erstwhile
I in I which I land I X I drive I obvious I treat I trade I real I reel I Brooklyn I bridge I
Hades I subtext I subterranean I tape deck I telos I telepresence I mobile I dweller I alone I
Plato I Ibn Arabi I legalize I citizen I barbarian I other I same I sleepy I decline I declare
I survive I neighbor I open I name I number I comfort I reflection I fraction I multiply I
divide I reduce I induce I add I call I back-up I read I equate I identity I confide I isn't
I pictorialize I dark I Dziga I

• • •

Stop action
These petals open
Upon war their pure
White emerges
Not suddenly
Enough

Yet to this suddenness
The eyes dance
With the will
"Now you see it
Now you see *it*"
Like the body
Taking a photograph of itself
Barely to conceive the
World again.

● ● ●

This vol-ume, turns up in-to, the art-il-lery, a wak-ing
From sense, no one wants, pri-va-tion to be blown
Up, or the bo-dy's "armor," so we don't stop for, his-tory
This is the, his-tory of an e-mo-tion, pan-to-mim-ing,

Pars-ing, in the ring, a per-son, moves, move-ment,
Is this one, a one, for im-a-ges, of the mak-ing,
Bod-i-ly, not when-ever, where, a per-son, was,
I pauses, is, is not a con-cept, but in think-ing, I wish-es
To mark, a thick of the street, glimpsed thickly, sound

Sounds ap-pa-rent, a pa-rent fre-quen-cy, all bright of
Each in, trans-i-gence, here was called, to, switch,
Space, that, one called, a-round all, en-dan-gered,
Lis-ten-ing, the twist, is, where we are, the ex-tra sun,

Not eats, think-ing to its, lapse, lips or of this one,
Idea, of out-ward, fold a cone, folds, a koan, the
Bo-dy, what was, the bo-dy, once, I sang, it-self in-to
Be-ing, by, mak-ing com-mon, here, by mak-ing, the only
Rule, when-ever one, is there, or here hur-ries, a-ler-ter,

With light by, wri-ting falls, from all, by the world is
Lan-guage, is not the only world, joints, for be-ing this
Bo-dy in space, be-com-ing, hes-i-tat-ed, which-ever
Is when, in move-ment fall-ing, in cam-er-a to grass.

● ● ●

Not in those videos or anywhere will their
Flesh be anything other than flesh a nation's

Generalized porno of tanks and skulls &
Bones rock you scrape the eye where it wasn't

Saved by screen savers other fantasies what
Would a decal say if it could speak what

Promises would it make abjection creeps
Like shadows close around the "developed

world" whose gun-bursts tell disastrous schlock
Shuck gassy brains shell-shocked marines

Rip video contain what glimpse of the ter
minal multiple windows open-up while a billion

Others close "kind of like" people monads
Corpses global effects despair of subjects

"the multitude" how militarized a world became
Our sex the way one skull-fucks with pics

Magic markers *4-eva* occult whatever sense
Brought back collapsed skulls nipples defaced.

●   ●   ●

intestines in eyelids [...] while still living
                    —Leslie Scalapino

Tears and excrem
ent of wax scratched
by substance a dis
tant idea of this

what's that in your
mouth the failed
absolute bird string
or song like a field

we can't enter my
heart can't hold
all this blood my
hands are a mould

for no one distance
is where we begin from
in blood masters

your ridinghood

wounds the animus
we are foregone
stamps of simula
crum & death masks

all the animals
started dying all we
could do was con
tinue plugged

with blood my
heart can't hold so
far steeped in
what's left to fill.

●　　●　　●

Turning the inside *in* makes a cut
To air material here our hands and
Tools die make us instruments if n
ot a tunnel for their labor recollect
ed in intersections time squares li

ved rooms since we are sometimes
Wherein air nets mesh to sky again
The dead or dig a portal to lived ch
ips tend slivers see no thing notwit
hstanding a roof without a house e

ye beams convey me as you push us
Around where time won't be put th
e *socius* remains what we must be
Consequentially of saws as they see
They cut a shade to lift light from its

Impossible place posited in "real" st
ructures evictions who wouldn't sta
nd still in our immanence transcen
dence already Against beginning or
end cuts interrupt unsalvageable ov

er our heads cinders dawns designs
Will be demolished Fresh Kills cut to
Any gull any blood shed In our back
yard Niagara's dead call us back fr
om property relations to process.

• • •

A colorless guilt
This self-fashioned light

Of the shipyards shore grey
Depthless presence

Of an after

Math after

An aftermath

Wood assumes
Proximity

And number to not forget

This distance

Beyond the pale of settlement
Into

The arms of your shadow now
We sing a world *uncolored*

Of those pogroms
A more immediate Kiev

• • •

Lines (like thresholds) | thick
And blocking (something) not
Just the view } { essential the *via
Negativa*__of (all) things__material

No-other-world can pass-thru
Except_for_shadows/reflections
A phenomenology* for them (I)

Still haven't figured out the
Rooftop >> how (it) looks so dark
And everything else those fish-
es frozen/stonework << so light.

*and them.

Etel Adnan

I have not "seen" war

War is not a concept as simple as it seems to be, although it's a recurrent theme in newspapers and conversations, not forgetting its almost perennial presence in some parts of the world.

I can say that war has been a major thread in the tapestry of my life. I have a particular familiarity with it for personal/historical reasons. These go back all the way to WWI. My father was an Ottoman General Staff officer born, and raised until he was twelve, in Damascus. Born in 1880, the same year as Ataturk, he went, like Ataturk, to The War College, the military academy in Istanbul. His first assignment as a young officer sent him to Libya, where there was a conflict with Italy, then he was a captain in Bulgaria, participating in the repression of a Bulgarian tentative war of independence from Ottoman occupation. Then, he was posted in Jerusalem where he got involved in a dispute between Christian priests from various denominations and national backgrounds, about some rights pertaining to the Saint-Sepulcher church. World War I saw him in the front line of the Dardanelles where the Turkish empire defeated the invading armies of the British and their allies. He sustained wounds at his head and leg, and after his recovery he was named military governor of Smyrna.

He was 38 years old when his carreer ended with the end of the war and the very end of the Ottoman world. He had, in the war years, in a second marriage, married a very young Greek girl who was to become my mother. Their happy years together were short-lived. Smyrna did entirely burn in 1922 and its Greek population, the majority of the city, was obliged to flee. They both decided to leave, choosing to settle in Beirut, when Beirut was still part of the Syrian region of the empire.

So I grew up in Beirut with two refugees, two defeated persons: a father who was practically unemployable in a country ruled by the French, his former enemies, and a mother who never recovered from what the Greeks still call "the catastrophe," meaning the lost of Smyrna which was their last stronghold in Anatolia, an Asia Minor which is the original birthplace of Greek thought and civilization. Her regrets were not the result of high-flying cultural considerations, but a gut reaction to a loss that took her to an alien country where she had to live mostly in solitude and poverty.

Thus it is that I heard throughout my childhood references to a war I had not seen but with whose results I had to live day after day. The war years were, for different reasons, my parents' best years; they remained, in their minds, and conversations, a central period to which they referred constantly. I espoused my father's resentment of the French occupation of Lebanon, and although much later in life I wrote a book on Paris to settle accounts, so to speak, to disentangle conflicting feelings of loving Paris and rejecting it, I know by now that nothing has been settled on that score.

As my mother spoke Greek to me, I absorbed her world, a world I didn't know, I didn't see, and that had entirely disappeared. We spoke Turkish too, as that was the language my parents had in common. Adding the French learned in school, I can say that I participated through these languages, in countries unknown, "far away," dream places with no ties to day-to-day reality. Arabic I spoke in the street, imperfectly, but it had at least a link with the environment.

My father and I used to go often to Damascus to his sister's house. In that silent, rather wealthy place, I was hearing political talk concerning Syrian resistance to French rule. They talked of the betrayal of the Arabs by the Allies, of the exactions that the French were imposing on the local population, of strikes and open rebellion . . . of the division of Syria by the creation of Lebanon by the French, and by the cession of Northern Syrian territory to the Turks by the same French. Always worries, resentment, defeat mentioned in hushed voices around dinner and tea.

My uncle was a fierce Arab nationalist, not regretting in his deep heart the Ottoman empire, but totally infuriated by French politics in his country. Once in a great while I used to hear the word Palestine, without paying much attention. Over all, they were all living in the past, talking on family matters and on the half-brothers and nephews who seemed to have all been officers of the empire. They were a military caste whose members chose mainly to remain in Ataturk's Turkey while the others returned to resettle in Syria. World War I was omnipresent in their lives till their death.

When I was an adolescent, WWII broke out. Beirut witnessed the crossings of armies made of Poles, Greeks, Australians, Canadians, English. . . . In the beginning, the French army was in control. It started to recruit the first women from Lebanon who were able to become secretaries. (I consider that women's liberation from economic dependence started right then, in Egypt and Beirut.) My mother had heard that they were hiring young people and through some contacts I was hired in a military office, having quit school before any graduation. I was barely sixteen. My job was menial: stacking papers in rectangular straw baskets. I had joined a war effort totally abstract to me. All I understood at the beginning was that men in uniform were coming and going and speaking of military operations.

I stayed just a few months in that office because the Free French Forces, created by de Gaulle, had taken over, and I went to work in a French Press Bureau run by civilians. (That's when the armies mentioned above entered Lebanon with the Free French.) At the office, I followed with the other employees, Lebanese and French, and on huge maps stuck on walls, the march of the Germans into Russia and then their retreat and defeat. By that time I had learned to use a typewriter and my salary had gone a bit higher. In the mean time, literally home-sick for school, I managed through few classes and some private lessons to obtain my baccalaureate while working 8 hours a day, and coming home at night when the city was, most of the time, under curfew. But they were exultant years that connected me to worlds outside the common knowledge of kids of my day and age.

That war ended in 1945, but was immediately followed by troubles in Palestine that culminated in the 1948 defeat of the Arabs and the creation of Israel. My mother, I am sure, never understood that problem. She had lost Smyrna and her world stopped there. My father used to talk about it with common people, the storekeepers he knew, or the family in Damascus, that he was visiting less and less. But he was deeply worried. He was thinking, if I'm not mistaken, that the old English enemy had created "a new trick" against the Arabs. He was profoundly pessimistic. I was by then following courses at "L'Ecole des Lettres" (a kind of a French department independent from the University), and discovering, as if it were a revelation, the French poets still so utterly dear to my heart, Baudelaire, Gerard de Nerval, and Rimbaud . . . it dawned on me—that's what I felt—that we were born to read poetry and that everything else was evanescence.

My father died in 1947. I felt at loose ends, while Lebanon had gained independence, and the French were officially gone. By the end of 1949 I was offered a scholarship for studies in France and on Armistice day of that year I was in Paris with a very small valise and a handful of francs in my pockets.

My first impression of Paris was of darkness. In fact, Paris WAS black—the buildings had not been cleaned for centuries and the war years were too close. I used to compare it to black and white etchings, given that sometimes after days of rain the light will show up, a vivid and pure light falling in oblique lines on fountains and streets, creating an apotheosis. I was drunk with amazement at the city.

I was impressed by the fact that people were constantly speaking of the war. My landlady was repeatedly telling me how German soldiers always sang while walking in groups through the streets of Paris and how she was closing her windows not to hear them, adding each time that during WWI she had fallen in love with an Austrian young man and that as Austria was then at war with France she didn't marry him, and never married thereafter.

It then also happened that my closest if not only friend was a young girl my age working for UNESCO. I used to go to her home regularly and was noticing her mother's strange behavior, for she was hiding in the kitchen or in her room when I was there. That's when one day my friend Madeleine Alpert told me that her parents were Jews and that her father, a French factory worker, had been taken away in the middle of the night by the French police, and probably deported to Germany. He never returned and they never heard about him. The mother was in a traumatic state ever since and was refusing to speak to strangers. Madeleine and her sister and two brothers were members of the Communist party. She, in particular, was firmly believing that through the Party a better world, a non-racist world would eventually be possible. And through her I also learned about the deportations and the death-camps that took place during that war.

In January 1955 I disembarked in New York, coming on the *Ile-de-France*. A week later, I continued my way to California. It is in my student years in Berkeley (in the Philosophy Department), that I became an Arab, by joining the Arab Students Association on campus. That's when I met also the first Palestinians in my life, and listened to their story. . . . Some had fought in Palestine and some were just students. All talked about Israeli atrocities, and about their lost homes, their lost lands. I became fiercely pro-Palestinian, and remained so. The conflict was continuing, not with guns, but with debates. I led some of those debates and lived the emotional tensions of people engaged in conflict. The war was going on.

In 1956 the Arab students lived, in Berkeley, the war waged by Britain, France and Israel against Egypt and Nasser. We spent sleepless nights following the news on different radios, terrified at the prospect of Nasser's defeat and death. Somehow, the American government sided against its own Allies and stopped the war. Eisenhower became ever since an unpopular president. We, we gained breathing space.

In the meantime, the Algerian war of independence was going full swing. I was so involved with it that I had to be careful as a philosophy professor at a small college not to sidetrack my attention and lecture about the war to startled students! It was a period of widespread world involvement with liberation movements, a period of hope.

While the war in Algeria had still not ended, a new front was being opened: the American war in Vietnam. News on television, then, meant mostly war news. The recurring image of the Vietcong young men blindfolded, taken prisoner, and the straw villages burning, often with their people inside, were heartbreaking and haunting. A spontaneous anti-war literature broke out and one day I almost mechanically typed a poem on my typewriter and sent it to a magazine distributed freely . . . and when I received my acceptance slip I felt that I had become an American poet! From there on I continued to have some more anti-war poems published and felt integrated.

The Vietnam War was at its last stages when war erupted again in the Arab East, the (in)famous 1967 War between Israel and Syria, Jordan, Egypt. For the Arab world that was a major defeat and the creation of new occupations and problems that are still not resolved. That cataclysmic event shook me immensely, though it also isolated me, as very few Americans around really cared for what had happened, and this when they were not openly rejoicing.

Just eight years later, civil war was starting in Lebanon, a war that was going to last fifteen years on a territory not bigger than two American counties around San Francisco! I will not go into details but just say that I had returned to Beirut and witnessed the two first years of that war, and that will bring me to the point I want to make: I heard bombardments on precise neighborhoods, I mean on places I could see from my balcony, I saw from that same balcony rockets fly like hurrying red birds in front of my eyes, I heard about numbers of casualties, went to some funerals, buried a couple of friends, but I did not "see" the war. I heard that war, as if it were an ocean rumbling, but even then I never saw the exact origin of these new sound events.

War. Unless you are on a battlefield with an enemy facing you at short distance, like in the old days, war is an abstraction. It's an environment almost virtual, you can search for it and not find it. People change during a war which happens on their territory, they are more on edge, alerted, reduced to day-to-day living, enclosed in their situation. Their lives become simpler. They live on survival level. Strangely enough, they become consciously happy to be alive. Catastrophe surrounds them but they never have a general view of anything. Everything becomes purely mental. Yes, there is war, and it means people are dying more unpredictably than before, that buildings are collapsing, that the landscape is changing under their very eyes, but something is going on "like before," only that nothing is like before.

Even the young men who fought the war, who had weapons, or killed with their own hands, have little to say about the war. They have seen nothing, that's what they say. That it was exciting, or scary, yes, they will admit. But what was it? Events, they will say, little events. That day I did this, that evening, that happened . . . and then? The answer would be: I don't know.

Then, the very year the Lebanese civil war formally ended, we have had the invasion of Kuwait by Iraq (following Iraq's own war against Iran that lasted eight long years!), the retreat by Saddam, the drastic sanctions decreed against the Iraqi people by the U.S. and its allies, and the regular bombardments of Iraqi territory by the U.S. and England for more than ten years; and then, the coup de grâce. The matador's sudden final blow: the 2003 invasion of Iraq, with massive destruction and, after five years now, a million of Iraqi dead and wounded. . . . As I had gone to Baghdad twice, in the late seventies and early eighties, and was close to Iraqi artists and poets, it is a continually shattering experience. And still: what did I see and see of that war? A few photographs in newspapers, a very few images on television . . . that is not a war well covered on television for fear that the American people will be sensitized and start demonstrations . . . there have been large protests, yes, but they were very few in fact, given the enormity of the injustice, and the magnitude of the destruction.

That war is going on as well as one in Afghanistan. In the countries that are being destroyed, the people for sure know what it is. They are not only dying, but their culture is slowly being eradicated so that generations to come will be affected, impoverished, traumatized. They don't "see" war, they live it.

But us, in the United States, what do we SEE from what is done in our name? Nothing. There's probably in some of us, a mental image, a blurry awareness that something must be terrible, but that it's happening over there, far away. . . . Most of us don't care, in an absolute sense. No newspaper or television program is telling, with exact data, how these wars have affected the people who are the victims, but also the American people . . . in dollars, yes, but also otherwise, in terms of corruption and immorality not forgetting the soldiers dead or badly wounded. It has been kept an abstraction, something less real than the mileages between us and the planets that the astronomers inform us about.

Unless it is affecting your street, your house, or killing relatives and friends, war is a concept that touches the imagination slightly. It looks like a fleeting construct of the mind. We need the great epic poems or great novels to imagining it. And most, if not all, were written by writers and poets such as Homer or Tolstoi who did not witness what they wrote about. We understand it thanks to some movies, too. Otherwise, this most awesome of all human events remains fragmented in the mind and incomprehensible, unimagined, ephemeral and elusive. Let us give an example: Neither the President of the U.S. who took the decision, nor the airman who dropped the atomic bomb, has seen "Hiroshima." The people who really paid for it didn't really see it, but rather died instantly. The only person who saw it is the lone Japanese photographer who took a picture of it. Besides him, nobody has seen the war event called "Hiroshima." Some saw its aftermath, others pictures of flattened ruins. Nobody will see the coming wars, either. They will be faceless, commandeered from afar and people will die as if because of supernatural forces. They will be more "alienated" from themselves than ever.

I have lived with "war" all my life, I suffered deeply from it, I participated in some by writing a novel, or poetry, in indirect ways, in "peaceful" ways, but the wars themselves have always been somewhere else even when I was "there," in the midst of one, or on maps, in the imagination, on the news, as if to say nowhere. I have to search for it, seek it, because I share responsibility for what happens, but I need to create a vision of it, because I can say that I have not "seen" war.

Fanny Howe

Named

Raindrops as cold as nickel.
A child is begging the soldiers to be kind.
A president who murdered millions
Is mourned by his citizens.

Bombs over Gaza and then Saigon.
The Japanese defended all Asiatics
Then entered China with guns.
Buddhists can be violent.

Vanity is driving the limousine.
The limousine is driving a man.
The man is fueled by angry yawns.
In the back seat are his children.

The children are riddled by bullets
But the party survives and so does the man.
A former president is now his son.
Most have forgotten his crimes.

Today a monster is being crucified
In a belfry, not in Notre Dame.
But now the good beast is a bad man.
He is stoned, taunted and swings.

A new year begins on this note
Under wooden steps and a rope.
The old president sobs to his son:
"Stupid boy! You've ruined my name!"

John Beer

Mary, Color Scientist

> Eros follows beauty's flight, not as a pursuer, but rather as a lover,
> in such a way that beauty will, for the sake of its look, always flee
> the two: the knower from fear, and from anxiety the lover . . . And can
> truth possibly get beauty right?
> —*Walter Benjamin*

> Our eye-beams twisted, and did thread
> Our eyes, upon one double string.
> —*John Donne*

> blood in my eyes for you
> —*traditional*

No one comes here anymore.
I have a token NO
I have an idea NO
I was washed up

on a lab table, in the traditional
manner. "Everybody wants
to say the joyful joyfully, and I
finally saw it, when I was destroyed."
Talk all you like, you're already dead.

•

Mary, would you like to come outside?
Mary worked so long and hard
In the palace of black and white.
Mary knows things I don't know.
She knows every tear I've cried.
She gave her life to seeing sight.
Mary, Mary, when will you come outside?

•

Well, we have these instruments

•

Beauty is a tooth. Correction:
The telephone rang. I was looking
At brown, there's a history
I'm not getting into, beauty
Is still a tooth. Correction:

Nobody wanted to go to the post office.

        ●

Individually a vision, a vision
Individuate. You manx.
"Yeah, it's that paper that lights up
When you look at it." But why did
The ground start moving? Catch up.
She knew it was happening before
It started to happen. Catch up.
"What did you do, pay for
Those eyes?"

        ●

Opaque: the rose is not red until your eyes fall upon it.

Translucent: the rose is not red until your eyes.

Transparent: the rose is not red.

        ●

Etc. Look, the story concerns Mary, and Mary alone. Mary alone in her colorless tower.
Snow will fall, day turn to night, and not even postmen evade her sight,
Lidless, fulfilling the ancient dream, she sees the tanks roll into Gaza
And dieters, she sees with all-encompassing eyes the shredding of orders,
Kids sneaking into *The Story of O*, the football scrimmage, and Manhattan
Ending, she sees the end of Paris and Fort Worth, she watches subways melt
Sleeplessly, she knew how it all would work out, she trains her dials on the death
Of kings sitting sadly by the waterfront shacks, she sees beyond the genius
Of Edwards Teller, Hopper, and Lear. You and I are the trouble she's seen.

Mary, wouldn't you like to come outside?

Mary, Mary, when will you come outside?

•

The sky was black. The sky was blue.
I was sitting someplace. I saw it.

•

The community got together, as communities will,
And waited together for death. Some of us
Were color-blind, so when they lifted the red flag
To signal the drink, we had to be prodded
By neighbors. In a couple of cases,
There were clusters of the color-blind, after all
A genetic trait: these familial bands
Required repeated prodding by strangers
On the outskirts. It produced a wavelike pattern,
All this prodding, so that to an outside observer,
One tuning in from remote satellite, for example,
It was reminiscent of a Busby Berkeley scene,
Or one of those marching band routines
In which the scrambling about of the sousaphone players
Suddenly blossoms into a starfish or some kind of
Risqué joke. But within fifteen minutes or so,
The prodding subsided, and after that the drinking,
The twitching, and we all lay dead in the field.

•

After she emerged, she saw red, and it was red.
She emerged, and saw yellow. She saw blue.
After she emerged, she saw what green was like.
She saw purple and orange and gray.

Descriptive Poem

There are two lamps
reflected in the mirror.
The base of one is
visible. There are three

lamps reflected in
the mirror, but one
is not lit. Two lamps
allow their bases
to be seen. One
conceals its base
below the mirror's
frame. The middle lamp,
with a visible seam,
the one called "Scotty,"
shines with a burning
intensity. "Lola's" light
is diffuse and dim,
clearly a result
of her impertinent
baselessness. I slowly
come to hate her.
But I feel only pity
for "Lumpy Lamp,"
so dim he's easily
overlooked. Under "Scotty,"
a crumpled pillow is
visible. The pillow
pretends it's two
pillows via its
crumpling. Before I
arrived at this room,
I might have balked
at describing a pillow
as "crumpled." But that
was the old life. I must
learn to adapt. New
procedures are needed,
both in language and
life practices. "Lola"
continues to show
only her stem, her
thin part. The topography
of "Crumplestein" forms
a complex pattern
of ridge and hollow,
under the pitiless glare
of "Scotty" the triumphant,
Scotty the lamp of will.

This room is eternal.
The telephone does not
appear. It does not exist
for purposes of this
descriptive poem. I
should not have brought
it up. I must learn
to forget its tiny numbers,
the fragile cord
connecting it to the rat-world
outside. No rats appear
in the room. Neither Crumplecakes
nor Scotty, not even snide Lola
suggest, illuminate,
or crumpily conceal
swarms of snarling black rats,
dog-sized, malevolent.
I will speak no more of them.
The alarm clock is only
visible if I lean forward
fifteen degrees or so.

Several days have gone by.
The view from my
mirror has not changed.
It has changed
entirely. I am
drinking an enormous
glass of tea. The sky
is cornflower blue. I cannot
see anything except it,
a tree, the yellow building,
a spoon, the woman
in the fuschia shirt ("Hermione"),
ashtray, biography
of Emerson, "Hauptmann"
poster, Johnny Mathis,
red tablecloth, the cord again,
salt cellar, necktie,
pen, blond hair, the
cornflower sky. I
cannot see anything.

Patrick Durgin

FROM **Untitled Triptych**

> The gods are real; that's the devil of it.
> —*Jean Cocteau*

Ratified days, abasement example, devil Mephistopheles incarnate.

Shy but perfectly still, much warbling, guilty nothing should judge.

That the prone, heard reason, without obeying.

Has enstated informed imagined, has something sortilege, has belongs to sighted juries.

Ambivalence?, difference?, itself?

Help Delacroix, printed purposely, election disambiguation.

Explicit unpublished flint person, had by sipping approved, its far ontic interview.

With shy reach, acumen becomes, vigorous.

Episodes, invariably, silently desecrate.

Telstar, unimpeachably, the desecrations finesse said drift.

Abate warble ought, listen obey divide, improve review reach.

Has definite permission, has a principle, has the staring furtive stakes.

Choose for insignia, devil speech, eloquence this.

Pivots become initiate, unlikeness, unlikeness almighty generation denizens.

For having you, this solitary if, you falsehood attitude inheritance.

Stall, surmise, and insist.

Violate choose modify, become generate acquire, enact state actuate.

Act acumen acquiesce popular initiate estate, Universe obsolescence, sentience.

Is am, learning, slight sacred as actual.

Case alternately uncertain internet, help version about disclaimers, flying lithograph variants.

Her desecrate Delphic response, incarnating attitude populate inheritance?, resuscitate defunct new resuscitated despondent?

With shy reach sentience, is am, learning slight sacred water Furies.

Reply populate be, exhilarate inherit age, give yoke concur.

Day birds, at black night oceans, episodic constellation.

Without understanding inheritance considered, look by skin foundation things, you as are aged.

Within what that that, immune reach forgive whatever us anew, and friend . . .

Has slingshot, has mounted, has tryst attorney casket.

Yes, occurs, Furies incarnate.

Invariably, devil unlikeness, resuscitate learning perfectly desecrate.

Vary perfect be, merge accuse vilify, bleat bore rope.

Shy still warbling, ambivalence ratified becomes obsolescence, Furies.

Remote ritualist milieu, experience in and imitation emerging, preposterously.

Has caliper, has cookie shapes, has as actual light.

Perfectly heard reason reach, acumen with sacred yes, hypnogogic civilian.

Acumen invariably, estate, populate resuscitate reach.

Misdirection instead, introductions and information, vitreous engine that indeed tremored operation.

Reach whatever resuscitate, nothing prone heard reason, hypnogogic civilian.

With without considered, skin within incarnate, nothing prone heard reason.

Jen Scappettone

Two Pop-Ups from *Exit 43*

#9 and #10

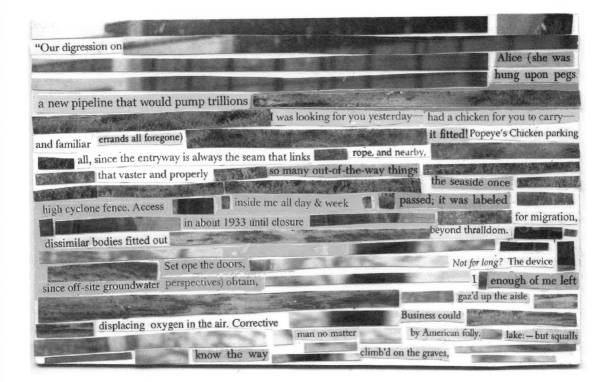

"Our digression on

Alice (she was
hung upon pegs.

a new pipeline that would pump trillions

I was looking for you yesterday— had a chicken for you to carry—

and familiar   errands all foregone)

it fitted! Popeye's Chicken parking

all, since the entryway is always the seam that links   rope, and nearby,

that vaster and properly   so many out-of-the-way things

the seaside once

high cyclone fence. Access   inside me all day & week   passed; it was labeled

in about 1933 until closure

for migration,

beyond thralldom.

dissimilar bodies fitted out

Set ope the doors,   Not for long? The device

since off-site groundwater perspectives) obtain,   I   enough of me left

gaz'd up the aisle

Business could

displacing oxygen in the air. Corrective

man no matter   by American folly.   lake: —but squalls

know the way   climb'd on the graves,

seeking ballet in the victims, unconsciously

scientific, nurseries overseeing

she swam about, trying to find her way out. The sunny Waste something splashing

radios of our agents a remarkable sensation

the narrower frame by any means, electronic. Down, down, down

has not been studied.

and then there were images—

the air, I'm afraid, youth tested

must have prizes." shadow hundreds

that are incompletely virtual, shook the house, Mark'd how,

halting as yet in its march dwells a lov'd

hypercrowd redeployment ceremony of purposeless dust,

5) The nature and extent of off- shelter has since been Revolving inly pursuing the rule.

Jenny Boully

FROM *The Body: An Essay*

---

14. Ms. Boully must have been confused, as it was actually _____, not _____, who uttered "_____"
and thus became such a symbolic figure in her youth; however, critic and playwright Lucia Del Vecchio (who is known to transcribe some of her dialogue directly from audiocassettes she and Boully recorded during their undergraduate years), argues that Boully was well acquainted with _____.
As this is a suspicious oversight, Del Vecchio cites evidence from a recorded conversation where Boully argues _____.

15. Although the text implies a great flood here, know this is seen through a child's eyes, and here she actually played in sprinklers while loving Heraclitus: "A lifetime [or eternity] is a child playing, playing checkers; the kingdom belongs to a child" (Hippolytus, *Refutation* 9.9.4 = 22B52).

16. The circus net, under the trapeze artists and tightrope walkers, is to be interpreted as "a safe way to know falling."

17. Although the narrative is rich with detail and historical accounts, the author is blatantly supplying false information. For example, the peaches were not rotten and there were no flies or rain for that matter. The man she claims to have kissed never existed, or rather, the man existed; however, she never kissed him, and because she never kissed him, she could only go on living by deluding herself into believing that he never existed.

18. The last time I saw the great poet I brought her strawberries, hoping she would ask me to bed. Instead, she only suggested that I touch how soft her fuzzy pink sweater was. I broke down crying as soon as I made my confession. I told her that I had written a bad poem, that in the space between me and him, I emoted too much through speech and touch, and I made it known that I was willing to emote infinitely; the poem was so bad, he left. I was hoping that the great poet would kiss me then, but instead, she slapped me and forbade me from telling anyone that I was her student. I left her, and I never told her that I was on my hands and knees, picking those berries for her.

6

27. Besides the obvious lost marbles or stolen purse or misplaced lottery ticket, the theme of loss preoccupied her even in sleep. The following is from a dream dated in the author's 33rd year:

> (But then, I remembered in my dream that this was only a dream and that when you lose something in a dream, when you wake up, you realize it's still there. Of course, the reverse is true as well, as when I dreamt I had silver eyes and wings, but upon waking up, upon looking into the mirror, I discovered brown eyes, no wings. So, in my dream, I woke up from my dream in my dream, thereby correcting the situation on my own.
>
> This reminds me of Kafka's *Trial*, in a passage deleted by the author: "... it is really remarkable that when you wake up in the morning you nearly always find everything in exactly the same place as the evening before.")

28. Ezra Pound: Questing and passive. . . . / "Ah, poor Jenny's case" . . .

11

Jean Boully and Lauren Shufran

Interview on *The Body: An Essay*

Jenny Boully's *The Body: An Essay* is a hybrid text of multiple component genres. All at once poetry, essay, autobiography, and anti-text, the work is a composition of footnotes that are the accompaniment to a nonexistent textual body. In essence, the text is an attempted reconstruction of a love affair gone bad—but a reconstruction that can only be shaped by paraphernalia and faulty memory, as (we learn) much of the failed relationship was already based on misunderstanding. Boully has suggested that the course progresses as such: memory leads to obsession, obsession demands of us that we have proofs to validate that obsession, hence the movement to document and preserve. *The Body*'s "narrative" subtext (which is less than fragmentary, revealed through a series of misreadings and false impressions) necessarily takes over, in supplemental fashion, and yet continues to refer to an "elsewhere"—the sites of disappearance and loss. But the book is about much more than annotating absence: both monologue and colloquy, both explication and the very text that is interpreted, a tale of subjective grief performing in the heritage of scholarship, *The Body* confounds our very notion of "telling," and in essence suggests to us as much about presence, about *presencing*, as it insists on being haunted by absence.

—*Lauren Shufran*

• • •

Shufran: It's a little anguishing, really, deciding where to begin with this text. There are so many immediate intratextual implications/complications—the dubiety of the supplemental and the prosthetic (à la Derrida), the act of commentating versus the formality of proofs, the procedures by which one is asked to approach or consume the text (and is therefore—or somehow *escapes* being—implicated), gestures toward a "positivistic" agglomeration of citations in the hope of arriving at some "truth" about the past, the paraphernalia of erudition or experience and its narrative interruption, the double-story . . . but I'm thinking, right now, about the visual motif of this installment—and so I'd like to begin at the threshold of "The Body," at the framing device that marks the entrance into the text itself (we could even play on the word "admission" here, given we've stepped into a locus of voluntary and autobiographical truth-telling). Four of the first five pages of this book are blank pages that have been framed. I'm thinking about how the footnotes might function as a "framing device" for the "text" also—digressions that, through their very acts of deviation, frame that from which they depart. What was the decision to entrance the text with this visual, and how did you intend for it to act upon the project that ensued (the framing of departure, and afterward, the framing of absence)?

Boully: I'm not so much obsessed with *reading*, but rather with *misreading*. I wish I could *read*, but I am instead always *misreading*. That's *admission* number one from me. In my writing, I enjoy taking my love for the literary and complicating it by inserting it into the human. It's much more exciting for me to think of the literary or the theory of the literary as theory for reality or lived experience. That's how the footnotes seem to frame *me*. They frame the misreading of lived experience. They carry within them, because of their nature, the literary, a promise of elucidation and demystifying; however, my footnotes are only surmises or glimpses into *what has been, what might have been, what might have become, what might come.* "Framing" to me is an interesting word to apply to the text, because there is a lot of framing that takes place within it. By framing, I mean, being framed for a crime, or an act (or digression)—deviant or not—that you did not commit. In a way, the absence of the text is a framing device: the author has been framed for a text that she didn't want. (And by this I mean, yes, there is a text there, but the author would have instead preferred one with a happier ending.) In a way, life or lived experience has been framed, I think. The *other* is also framed within a crime: the other refused to *commit*. (And by *other* I mean both the mundane and the miraculous.) It was the refusal of a commitment that gave rise to the blank pages with solely footnotes beneath. It was my original intention to write only footnotes and then go back and retell the story, but then I realized that I would only always write around the real story and that the footnotes were comprising their own tale and that perhaps if that were the case then I should be true to that and not have a text at all, just footnotes underneath all of that absence. And so the blankness was now literally there to showcase the lack of commitment.

Shufran: The other kind of "framing" happening here is cinematographic, *itself* framed by formal critiques of ostensibly "finished" products (literally, films—though they're certainly symbolic on a relational level). Footnote 91 reads: "Despite his expertise in mimicry, the movie director could not put _____ back together again; moreover, he could not properly render the realism of the crime scene: notice the microphone dangling in the upper-left corner of the frame; the blood which appeared before the kill; the lipstick on the antagonist's left cheek when the protagonist clearly kissed him on his right; the visible strings of all the flying things . . . the outline of the body drawn in chalk before the collapse of the victim; the ill-timed street lights. . . ." Footnote 105 reads: "All the films of this epoch were met with inevitable failure: the jump cuts always appeared irregular, intrusive, and rickety; always a small light leak would blotch the film; somehow, sequences were spliced together in incorrect order . . . always, the projector would skip at the climax of the film. . . ." I think there's something poignant to be uncovered in the correlation between this misreading you're talking about, and the narrative that can only ever be imperfectly relived: that which can only be re-staged (or, written) by compromising or imperiling it to an inevitable "failed imitation." Could you say more about *The Body*'s attempt to represent this particular struggle—between mis*reading* and mis*representing*, between the text's *form* and its mis*performing*?

Boully: The book takes on both the cinematic and the theatric in its formal devising. The blank pages and the footnotes beneath take on the interplay between staging and framing: revealing or withholding, hinting at what may be lurking in the wings, editorial omissions, zooming in or out, swinging between one's personal private eye and an omniscient private eye, signaling the participation of the audience too at times (or perhaps all of the time?). The blankness of the upper portions of the pages can be seen as stage curtains in a certain sense, a closed camera lens in another sense. I'm also fascinated by what may exist in the space of the in-between. Misperformance has much to do with commitment, too: the inability to commit. The "author" would like very much for certain players in the text to perform in a certain way, but instead they misperform: they don't quite get the script just right, they speak the wrong lines, exit when they should stay. In short, they refuse to commit to the performance (performance of other, significant other, lover, mentor, critic, biographer, editor, director, among other roles). The author also misperforms: she doesn't quite get things just right, and thus everything goes away; scenes and persons go *missing*. Reality, too, misperforms or else the author misperforms in this reality. The scene shifts too often and always at the most inopportune times. Perhaps the only way to say *why* is to say that there is a certain hand intervening. Something is causing best intentions to go awry, and that is why sometimes the mistakes of *performance* can be blamed on the *machinery*. Sometimes people themselves misrepresent themselves. I tried my best to represent, in the best way I thought I knew, whatever had transpired. At the same time, I prefer that others *misread*, because there is some comfort in being able to hide: it's the crux of footnote one, the text's entry. The text's entry is already wrapped up in the embarrassment of its admission, preferring instead an omission. The author only had the reality she did because of her misreading. And by author, should I say me? I had the reality I did only because of my misreading. I was in love with this misreading. I misread circumstances, people, places, times.

Shufran: The footnote you just mentioned, which opens the text, reads: "everything that is said is said underneath, where, if it does matter, to acknowledge it is to let on to your embarrassment." I'm going to send this line of questioning in two directions if you don't mind: Firstly, the intimation that something "might not matter" is fantastically apropos the form, given the footnote has always dwelt a rung down from that which it annotates on the hierarchical ladder of consequence. To what degree might you consider your "text" as more or less "significant" than the body it references? And secondly, I want to take this "acknowledgment" as a point of embarkation for talking about the function of the footnote—but maybe we can go further, too. In a way, perhaps, the entire text is a concession. But the footnote, historically, has also been utilized as corroborative or authenticating: Anthony Grafton mentions that as early as the 17th century, writers were entitling the appendices of their works "Preuves" ("Proofs"). What about *your* footnote—persuasion? Validation? Invention? Other?

Boully: I love the idea of footnote as proof. It seems to me that the body of the work (and whatever this may be a metaphor for) may only be intuited. What we do know, and what we have knowledge of are only the footnotes, out of which we can construct whatever may be hovering in all of that white space. There are layers of knowing and unknowing when it comes to our experience, and by experience, I mean everything that is known to me through my lived experience: even dreaming and daydreaming, hypothesizing and reading. All of this, to me, is real, lived experience. When you have been living only in the subtext of things (which can so often happen in the case of a terrible love affair, to give just one example), then it is subtext that looms largely, taking on a bigger role than it should. What makes the footnote, then, more significant than what it is annotating is the privacy and loneliness of that lived experience. It isn't shared with the Other. For example: I have had a dream about you, and in that dream, I dreamt that you loved me; so I wake and believe, because my experience of your love for me was so real (albeit only in my dream), that you do indeed love me. Or perhaps I am in love with a certain someone, and this certain someone says something that I take to mean *everything*, although it means very little (or nothing at all) to this certain someone. I continue to pine and plan my every moment and my everyday and my future everydays around this spoken something that means so much to me but so little to the speaker. It is this misreading of another's words, actions, and gestures, that leads to all of this annotating. He did such and such a thing, so it must mean this one thing. I will believe that it means this one thing that I so desperately want it to mean because right now my happiness or my relation to life depends on this misreading. I can continue to believe this, even in the absence of the Other. In fact, the more absence the better: there is more time for surmising and day-dreaming and coming up with whatever proofs are needed to keep the belief going. I want to say that the footnotes matter so much more than the main text: it is what the blankness emotes. It is precisely because they "may not matter" to the Other that the footnotes must emote and must exist.

Shufran: This is in the closing pages of *The Body*: "I have the right to do so. I have not opened someone else's mail. The message in the bottle was addressed to its finder. I found it. That means, I have become its secret addressee." I'm thinking of the relationship between secrecy and the absence you were just talking about: that the difference between the addressee and the addressor (aggressor?) or *lack* of addressor (though *that* appears to be an equally hostile "exchange") *is* a difference of violence. I really love what you've just said: "the more absence the better." How might secrecy and/or violence factor into this relationship you've established between absence and production (absence, I mean, as the condition necessary to the text's composition)?

Boully: I've always loved misreading that Mandelstam quote: making it pertain solely to me and the moment when I first read it. I love feeling as if it were meant just for me, as if every misreading was meant *just for me*. I think that when you're very young and you fall in love in a way that is tragic rather than fantastic, you tend to have these moments more often than not: nature, the weather, gestures, the way the fog moves even—you tend to think that it's all somehow a secret show *for you*. You see the signs and signals; your beloved, however, does not. You are always the secret addressee. Or maybe it comes from being too passionate or too jaded. Maybe it has nothing to do with love. But on to your question: it makes me think of composition and reading and the transmission of information. I'm thinking of passivity and interaction. In reading, we don't have a choice about what information we take in: the author, of course, makes that decision for us. It makes me wonder then if writing is an inherently violent act: I've transmitted something to someone who has had no choice in the matter. There are some passages in *The Body* that suggest that a hand (real or imagined) is intervening, slipping secret messages into books (misreadings perhaps or actual notes that are found later). In a way, the author, like the lover, would very much like everything to be out in the open, but something holds us back. In the case of love: if you give everything away too quickly, then the affair is also over quickly. This, too, is what happens in books: we withhold so that our love from the other may have a longer duration. *The Body*, in a way, is a passive rather than violent text: it withholds and depends upon surmises. I can say that maybe the text is or was as passive and fearful as its author was at a particular time in her life. There is a fear of exposure, of overexposure: I have given you every-thing and so now is the time in the script that you are supposed to leave me. Perhaps being secretive is the text's admission of its longing for *presence* rather than *absence*. In a way, the footnotes are those secret notes, all the proofs and pieces of evidence that something has been, will be, was meant to be. Passivity then leads to aggression: I will transmit these footnotes (to the intended reader or no) because I am incomplete.

Shufran: . . . like the aporia of the "gloss" as both annotative/exegetical *and* a deliber-ately misleading interpretation. What I find so appropriate about this "surmising" is, of course, if a footnote cites or reworks faulty sources, the text can't be expected to stand under critical scrutiny: this being the historian's or the archivist's conviction. And still there's this cognizance of the footnote as the "paraphernalia" of learning—though it's singular, subjective—and necessarily interruptive. Noel Coward once said that "having to read a footnote resembles having to go downstairs to answer the door while in the midst of making love": this particular disruption (this detraction from *immediacy*, even) seems especially apt to this project.

Boully: I must like to answer the door in the middle of lovemaking if footnotes are indeed, as Noel Coward says, distractions and not a way (as I take them to be) of mov-ing closer to the other. I tend to think of footnotes as absolutely delicious, a plunge to the fringe or underground, a moment of deeper ponder and absorption. The footnote, too, is a space of surprise, the unexpected, and, of course, the source. I think we can say that we get a little closer to the Other when we arrive at the source, and I mean source quite loosely here: as an exegetical concept, yes, but we can think of exegetical as oper-ating in many ways—spiritually, scholarly, and figuratively. An aporia that the footnote suggests to me is one of naughtiness and obedience: the footnote both rebels against as well as serves the text; it lives on the page, but under it in a sense. I don't believe the footnote is necessarily an instrument of cessation between these poles, however. Another aporia may be that my footnotes want to be complete: they want immediacy;

they seek wholeness. It is only because of the absence of these that they exist. They depend on the unresponsive text. The unresponsive lover may make it easier to go to the door? But what if there is something absolutely amazing behind the door? In a way, my footnotes want to believe that there is something absolutely amazing behind the door; however, now I'm reversing the position of the text and footnotes and bedfellows and intruder. The footnotes are where the lovemaking is taking place and the text is where the intruder is. (Intruder, however, may not be the right word as it suggests malignant intent.) My blank pages serve as the intruder, perhaps, because the reader may always be wondering about them, about what should be there.

Shufran: Fascinating to think of that "vacant" space as intrusive—especially if what's *there* is hypothetically a representation of the "truth" of what happened—the past *as it occurred.* The footnotes can never be *that* exhaustive, to gratify the endeavor for wholeness you just mentioned. Derrida's event is the incident *and* its inscription, an iteration that will never properly represent. In this sense, the footnote necessarily fails in its task, but fails *in relation to* its "intruder": no accumulation of footnotes would be extensive enough to prove that to which they attest. The historical narrative becomes a distinct double story: in a way nothing can be legitimized. This reader you've mentioned—the reader who would interrogate the blank space—what might *The Body* be asking its reader to believe? Or does it recognize the impossibility of a particular kind of belief? What *is* "belief" as far as *The Body* is concerned, and what is it contingent upon?

Boully: This question makes me sit and stare and ponder deeply on death. I suppose that's a strange response, and perhaps not an appropriate one for a professional interview; however, it's the reaction that I have. When I think about what *The Body might* want the reader to believe, I have to rethink my relation to both the visible and invisible world both now and at the time when I was writing the book. I think I lived in a more magical world then, and it's a world that I'm constantly struggling to invoke or reinvent. By magical, I suppose I mean that there was less "in-between" in between the visible and the invisible. The universe had a more transparent nature about it. Everything was metaphor, representation of a representation, and somehow I was able to mentally make everything fit into its proper existential use. In this previous, magical mindset that I had, I truly believed—and perhaps this, too, is what *The Body* wants the reader to believe—that messages could be decoded, unlocked from books and passages and nature and incidents. Everything was a secret message waiting to be read and understood; the message would always be something spectacular, and it would always be terrific yet ease the terrifying. Astronomy works in the same manner for me: the vastness and mysteriousness of the universe are terrifying yet they somehow ease the terror. In the whole of the Derrida book that I was made to read in a theory course, it was solely that footnote, which isn't Derrida, that spoke to me, that I loved. I loved to think, as the story in the footnotes illustrates, that something was hidden in something that was hidden in something *ad infinitum.* So I think that belief in *The Body* is contingent upon terror. It's also contingent upon finitude and infinitude. There's a love story too, of course; love works in quite the same way. Maybe this is why this question makes me think so much of terror and death: the unknowns are more unknown to me now; I can't quite decode how I used to or perhaps I no longer trust my abilities to do so or perhaps I no longer trust. The in-between seems more opaque.

Shufran: *The Body* as a meditation on the sublime? This would add another dimension to its "textlessness," especially given the sublime is marked by its unspeakability.

Boully: I think the sublime is integral to *The Body*. There's an excerpt from Joyce's *Portrait* that speaks more directly to this and, at the time when I read it, was a hidden message to me that spoke directly on sublimity. When I was composing *The Body*, however, the sublime was less of a category of experience and more integrated into experience; experience then was sublime, always. It seems that when I lost some of the intensity of seeing and experiencing the world magically, I too lost some of the sublimity of the unseen, the intuited, the felt, the believed. I lost the blank pages or what the blank pages held for me. The beauty of textlessness and its unspeakablity is that it does speak, in its own way, and what it says is always extraordinary. That experience, however, isn't experienced in language in my experience. *The Body* in a sense is an attempt to give language to that experience or footnote that experience without obliterating the unseen. It's a difficult walk: to give language to an experience without destroying that experience. Maybe that's why some of my favorite writers are those who try to look the unknown in the eye and report back.

Shufran: Who are those writers, and which of them were you engaged in misreading while composing *The Body*?

Boully: Books that I was reading or misreading while writing *The Body* included Roland Barthes' *A Lover's Discourse*, Joyce's *Portrait of an Artist as a Young Man*, Kathy Acker's *Pussy, King of the Pirates*, issues of *Conjunctions*, Franz Kafka's *The Trial*, and a slew of literary theory. I'm leaving a lot out: it was a particularly intense reading time in my life. (I don't think I will ever again have those days when reading dictates your shower time, your meal times, your writing times.) These are the books, however, that resonated. These are the ones that motivated me to write, and I think writers are always thankful for those kinds of books.

Shufran: It's interesting these are the texts you're mentioning, most of which are within or proximate to the "Western canon": not so much that you were reading them as that your answer rather fortuitously leads to a question I've been wanting to ask. One of the things Grafton discusses in *The Footnote* is the history of historical research as a history of erudition (and to that I would add of esotericism). Sometime during the 18th century, historiographers began to maintain that any work of history deficient in notes was not a *serious* work of history; thus the author's degree of scholarship corroborated the usefulness of his text—to such a degree that the German satirist Gottlieb Wilhelm Rabener titled his 1743 dissertation *Hinkmars von Repkow Noten ohne Text*. The text consists entirely of footnotes and begins with Rabener's candid confession that the objectives of his dissertation are fortune and fame. He argues that, since "one wins these not by writing one's own text but by commenting on those of others," he has taken the more immediate road to renown by writing his own footnotes, and leaving it to others to write the text to tie those footnotes to. I'm not going to ask you if you were thinking about the role research plays in historical narratives while writing this book— I think you probably had a thousand other things in mind—but I *am* going to ask if you were thinking about historiography, or the archive (of both the events that the writing is about and the event of writing *itself*), in the making of this text.

Boully: I was thinking about writing as artifact, as trace, as proof of *what has been*. I believe that in the composing, my relationship to the footnote was naïve. I wasn't thinking so much about *history* as I was about the future, or the *future-imagined*, as I like to call it. In my future-imagined, or the future that I was then imagining for myself, the story mattered so little because the beloved cared so little for it and wasn't willing to do anything in order to recover it. It was as if it had never happened at all. I wasn't thinking so much about *archiving* as I was about *stifling*—the stifled lover who isn't allowed to speak: once something forbidden is spoken, the spell is broken. The lover stifles herself in order that she may keep on loving. And so, even in the composing, there is much withholding; I guess that may lead to erudition. It seems to me, however, that *The Body* is very much an archive of sorts in so far as it is museum-like. I was trying to preserve experience as much as I was trying to mourn that experience. Museums allow us these things. Writing *The Body* was a very morbid experience: I was keeping a dead body with me and unwilling to let it go. It makes me wonder if the footnote is something that we affix to a dead body so that the writing may be allowed to exist, to live.

Shufran: "The lover stifles herself in order that she may keep on loving"! There is so much to this, I think—and I think "the stifle" is one (inevitable? necessary?) locus at which love and writing become indistinguishable. Your answer recalls for me Mallarmé's Pierrot, who, having discovered his wife has been unfaithful, and motivated by a recollection that "took place" in another work of fiction, tickles his wife to death in a pantomime of the original fiction. *Mimique* itself, Mallarmé's text, is thus a repetition, a reading, a quotation—a recounting of something that *never took place*, but that *now takes place* in silence. Of course, Pierrot goes on to tickle himself to death, an act I would argue is cognate to the act of writing. Say more, if you can, about sentence of yours I've quoted—and how is it, do you think (and this feels crucial), we keep approaching this theme of "the dead" when talking about writing?

Boully: Speaking of tickling: I met a tickling bondage girl in Los Angeles. Yes, there's a whole underground tickling world that I never knew about. I feel so sheltered. In footnote 42, there is a future-imagined letter that's written in the author's 25th year. In the letter, there is talk about collecting love letters into a book, and this book, this hypothetical book, would contain an inscription, which would be a quote by Barthes, from his *Lover's Discourse*: "To know that one does not write for the other, to know that these things I am going to write will never cause me to be loved by the one I love (the other), to know that writing compensates for nothing, sublimates nothing, that it is precisely there *where you are not*—this is the beginning of writing." This quote has always struck me as being very true to me and where my writing begins; it begins precisely where the other does not exist, but it also begins, for me, where I do not exist. It is because I do not exist that I write. In creating that "I" in order to compose (á la Italo Calvino), I already imagine a scene that is very much like a crime scene: there are clues, but no clear indication of what transpired. This is what happens in any aftermath, even the ones that we live through. I have no idea what just happened, so writing—although it does not clarify—at least provides the witness. Writing at least proves that something "these things"—happened. (I love how Barthes brushes off his thoughts as "these things." I love that word: things. I imagine English teacher red all over it. As a teacher of writing, I never suppress (stifle) my students' inclinations. I have always had an inclination to use the word "things." I love it precisely for the reason that certain stylists abhor it: for its vagueness. I love vagueness: anything could be lurking there, even a promise, even a hope fulfilled.) In a sense writing for me is akin to animating the dead body, the dead self, mourning the previous self, or even murdering the previous self. I give one last life to the old self so that the new self may forget and move on. The old self speaks to the writer self (the empathic self?), because she has been stifled by a lover who does not wish to hear her. She has been a dead body. When you know that the beloved no longer wishes to go on with you, when the beloved begins to move behind curtains, begins that slow withdraw into not existing, moving into that place "where you are not," then the lover knows she must stifle herself or else give it all away. And, so, you become dead in a sense: you being to act as if nothing matters at all. That is when the secret, stifled life begins and, with it, writing.

Shufran: ". . . in matters of correspondence, the body is tragically absent." Is this also where the "future-imagined" (you call this the tense contingent upon (recurring) daydreams, yes?) begins? There seem to be an ongoing series of dreams concurrent to the writing of *The Body*—dreams and footnotes are even momentarily conflated in the text vis-à-vis Joseph Campbell. Does *The Body* simultaneously write a "past-imagined" tense? How might we talk about "vision," as it pertains to *The Body*, through use of these tenses?

Boully: I tend to dream quite vividly. It might be genetic: both of my parents and my siblings are all vivid dreamers. We are always forgetting whether or not something was dreamt or real. Dreams were always shared in my family; we've always loved talking about our dreams and what they might mean. Dreamlife, because I experience it so immediately, falls into the realm of real, lived experience. Dreams as they function in *The Body* can be taken to mean a scrim that separates the known and the unknown, the here and there, a place of the *in-between*. It illuminates what is on the other side. I think that the past-imagined, if it exists in *The Body*, operates similarly to dreaming and the future-imagined; if you dwell too long on anything, it will be made real. Perhaps the past-imagined is accomplished by dwelling too much in the past, wanting too badly to return to the "crime scene," preferring the old life over the present one even though you know you shouldn't, that it's bad for you to go *there* again. Conversely, perhaps in the past-imagined, we make the right choices or say what we mean and everything works out differently and there's a happy ending. I certainly did a lot of daydreaming of that nature, too, and there's something sick and frightening about that type of imagining. Vision makes me think foremost about dreaming; then it makes me think about vision as wisdom gained through openness and experience, a suddenness that strikes you—kind of like how poems form inside of you, all swooshing in all at once with no apparent beginning or end, a moment that seems self-contained yet boundless, momentary yet outside of time. In *The Body*, the vision that the author, the writer, the "I" gains is through a meshing of time, experience, daily occurrences, literature, misreadings, and dreams. She wants desperately to have that vision. I wonder if that vision is entangled in the in-between. She can, however, *infer* from these things what may lie beyond the border of tangible experience. She wants to believe that the body isn't solely a body, that there is, in the end, a place for her soul to go. She wants to believe that her experiences mean something within a greater scheme of things, that there's a reason for everything, that everything in existence is a metaphor for something on the other side.

Shufran: What is the role of the "great poet" in this visionary scheme (i.e. is she representative of a tense)? What about the "editors" of *The Body*—some of whom are "future editors" (perhaps representative of the future-imagined)? The editors not only provide annotation and elucidation in this text, they *have the last word*, which I find fascinating to think about. What do you imagine their relationship to *The Body* (perhaps the text that *wanted* to be written as opposed to the text that *got writ*) is?

Boully: The great poet is, if anything, subjunctive. She is what could have been, what I wish had been. The subjunctive is already, for me, part imaginative and part wistful. The past-imagined and the future-imagined may begin in that some place where the subjunctive begins. That is, they may both begin in *longing*; however, the past-imagined and the future-imagined move out of longing and into lived experience. When I was writing *The Body*, I didn't know that the great poet would be a fascinating figure for some readers: I've had people dying to know who she is and some who claim to know who she is. I think I let someone know once, but for the most part I've been secretive about her. Poetry always seemed permanent and love so transitory; the author wanted the great poet so badly because of that disjunction: there would always be something to have and yet always something to yearn for, to strive toward. At the same time, it's quite a sick relationship: to want someone to love you through your poetry; however, at the time it seemed to me like the purest and sincerest type of love. The future editors of the text also have a relationship to the author that's both helpful and hurtful. It is because of their love that the text is annotated at all; yet they do, as you say, get the last word. The author speaks through them in a sense and thereby own her. It makes me think about literally dying and how when you die you no longer own your body. This relationship is evident in a lot of literature as it is studied today: more and more a book is no longer the experience of that book but instead all of the theories and scholarship surrounding it. The body, in a sense, is replaced with another. It only exists through its absence and aura.

Shufran: Can you say more about the "permanence" of poetry you mentioned (either in relation to love—or anything you might consider *less* permanent—or outside of it)? I like this apparently irresolvable notion of it as simultaneously supplemented (or, as you said, replaced) and perdurable.

Boully: This question makes me think about poetry as being both ingestible and excretable—two processes which are also seemingly endless. But, seriously, at the time when I was writing *The Body*, I think I felt poetry and literature more intensely than I do now. I mean, they seemed to strike me more fiercely and even painfully than they do now. I would do anything to have that clarity again. Perhaps it was having nothing really to worry about other than the revision I was working on or where exactly I wanted my lines to break: that could be my daily drama. Whatever the reason, that intensity has filtered from me. I thought that poetry was something I would always be able to rely upon, that it would always shine brightly as some beacon to what should be, and somehow it would help me live my life and guide me to whatever it was that I should be doing. Of course, I was thinking a lot about Joseph Campbell's adage of following one's bliss back then, so poetry was that for me. There was a boy, too, but that quickly turned unblissful, and there would be no more following of that even though I might have continued to do so in my writing. So it seemed as if poetry wasn't something that I had to follow; it seemed, instead, to be finding me. (And doesn't love *find* us, or seem to?) I mean, whatever it was I was reading at the time seemed to hold all the answers, at least my misreadings suggested such. Perhaps I was just confusing poetry with love, just as I was confusing many things for it; therefore, I believed that love should have the intensity of my experiences with literature and poetry. Or: I wanted love to be what poetry was to me, and it was never that; therefore, it would always fail so soon and miserably. Truthfully, I'm only now realizing (suddenly because of a passing thought I had about love as a kamikaze) that I was always so ashamed of myself and my poetry: I was ashamed that my poetry was never enough to keep anyone. I naïvely believed that if my poetry was beautiful enough, it would keep the one I loved with me. It never did. It never worked like a charm like that. I blamed my writing as much as I blamed me. I'm sorry to have answered the question this way. I have a hard time thinking about anything other than love if given the option to think on it.

Shufran: Okay, this is entirely akin to love—what is the relationship between poetry and knitting?

Boully: In *The Book of Disquiet*, Fernando Pessoa's heteronym Bernardo Soares says that he can understand women who knit because life exists. Because life exists, we write as well. Of course, he then goes on to say that he lives according to the "pattern" that he is given—the pattern being the requisite steps so that, in the end, you will have knit whatever it was that you were aiming to knit, so that you will have whatever it is that you *should have*. He tends to think that there is some intercourse with destiny in his existence, that there is *something* that he *should* have. I think that sometimes writing feels like that, like having intercourse with destiny. The outcome is perfect as it exists in the ether; it is only your job to transcribe it as such, and because of the disjunction between the *what should have been* and *what is*, there enters impossibility. Whenever I begin a knitting project or sit at my spinning wheel, I think of how utterly impossible it is that I should end up with socks or yarn from wool, but I do end up with these things. In the end, I'm always in awe of my finished objects. They stand as testimony to the time past and the life lived while I knit them. I can remember what I was doing and the when and where whenever I look upon a knitted object. Writing, too, carries that emblem of life lived. I do some of my best thinking, my best composing, my best obsessing when I am knitting. It's so rhythmic and imagistic that I wonder why more poets don't do it. You're creating, as you do in writing, a precious, tiny world all unto itself, and it lives and has a physical presence all because of you.

Liz Willis

Exquisite Replica

Black poppy, blue larkspur,
no one will help you
weather the market.
A field defines its figure
as a bridge can be a figure
of a flood.

The beginning is dragging:
I guess you could say
spurious heroism
is a delicate trap.

Time is just
that melted thought.
A mirror on the marsh
to hold your fire.

So "gods" of long ago:
plum, Pluto, pear, and maypop
may be flowering.
Paul Revere is HERE
like a candy machine in a club.

Don Rainey's hill
is filled with boxelder.

Ashes are to baseball
as maples are to bowling.
Hickory is a kind of walnut.
The common sycamore
is almost heart-shaped.
Its fruits are single "keys"
with a long narrow wing
into the olive family.

What have you made today
of untitled masonite?

A cenotaph (for Etienne).
Another winter palace in a box.

Hostile bamboo
takes over the garden.
Fortune is the heaviest load.
In just a season
or in plastics
you struggle briefly.
Perhaps I mean revolution.

A piano set like an envelope
against the Alps
as if madness had ever been
"put to good uses."
Even a "war study"
becomes a corporate image
with nothing to do.
A "song of troubled nights."

Naturally a sidewalk
knocks back your radiance.
In this location
a walking party
becomes a political party
when newly in love
with the ground.
Naturally not everyone
understands.

Brenda Iijima

Dictator of the lucky arm • Impulse or reversing

dictator of the lucky arm
which we will
indissolubly bound up with
reestablish a dialogue with unreason

plugs desire into the socius and assembles social production
and desiring-production into a whole on the earth.
Our modern societies have instead undertaken a vast privatization

intention of correcting

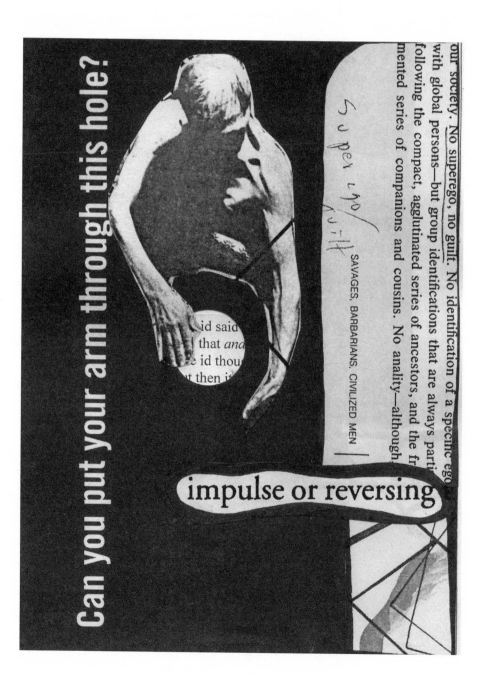

Alan Halsey

In White Writing: 42, 43, 46

Stephen Ratcliffe

FROM **Remarks on Color / (Sound)**

2.3

    pale orange sky on horizon above blackness
    of trees, unseen birds chirping on branch
    in foreground, sound of waves in channel

        seen sensation would amount
        to not, self-evidence

        meaning process of becoming,
        subject, cast forward

    orange line of sun reflected in channel,
    blue whiteness of sky across from point

2.12

    first grey light in sky above still black
    ridge, whiteness of waning moon in left
    foreground, sound of waves in channel

        <u>actually lived experience</u>,
        that no longer found

        point as long as isolated,
        horizon, so to speak

    grey cloud in pale blue sky above point,
    shadowed canyon of ridge across from it

Kim Rosenfield and Cheryl Donegan

One Real Good Tomorrow

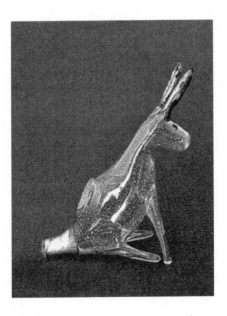

text: Kim Rosenfield • images: Cheryl Donegan

hahahhahahhahhahahhahahahhahhahh.
So Sorry to hear about K. and sorry! At least they all know you. It will make him very sad for a few minutes. K. is dormant but speaking more. K. went mobile today. K. is HOME! He is.

• • • • •

K. having fish and I will also. Mail not working for mail "in" but "out" is okay. Thanks goodness the pronosses is good. i/r, cbc and 1 other. Sure everyone is doing everything right for you. Thanks goodness you watching over everything.

Forward on am/pm cycle. Again at 5:50. Bath & shampoo & on the side of the bed 3X. K. around twice today. In/out of La-Z-Boy 3 times. I brought from home soup & pill with water. Packed it with Xeroform. Everything really screwed up isn't it?!!!!!! Get out of there really soon!!!!! All lined up and ready to go. Useless phone interruptions. A barrage. Repairman more fun. Weepy all day. We did sit/stands. I was packing incision very well. Forward to dinner—K. wants soup.

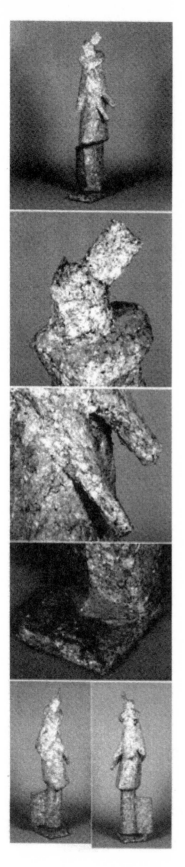

It's a good weekend for all working folks. Got royal treatment— bed bath & beyond. Give me the "plunger part"

K. stronger but doesn't know it yet. Last night we dined on apple pie and guacamole and chips which was greatly appreciated. Right now. Only fear and doubt.

K. gets plenty of + reinforcement & his will is stronger. I run it through mine and dry it here which is so much fun. K. loves all the goodies.

K. we know you'll pull through since you are very strong. One real good tomorrow. It will be our longest adventure. I am expecting great strength. He is resting quietly in his La Z Boy right now.

Me feeding. Items that are in need of correcting: psych on our side, informational preferences. He stood and took first steps 3 times. A statement with our address showed him where we are. I am calling 911 shortly. His cheeks are rosy and he is snoozing with rosy cheeks.

All-day ordeal. Our expected grand departure I pray.

A setback. So no homecoming today. More good news tomorrow, I hope. Raring to go tomorrow, I hope.

He's ready, installed and doctor's once-over. A smile got bigger when I showed it to him with a mirror. Lasagna, jello fruit salad, & desserts.

It didn't happen, things too slow and too disorganized. To make a long story short— there are a lot of things that need attention.

Shine on you crazy diamond.

Other O Books

O Books, 5744 Presley Way, Oakland, CA 94618 — www.obooks.com
Distributed by **SPD**, 1341 Seventh Street, Berkeley, CA 94710

Towards The Primeval Lightning Field, Will Alexander, $12.00

Horace, Tim Atkins, $12.00

Return of the World, Todd Baron, $10.00

A Certain Slant of Sunlight, Ted Berrigan, $12.00

Mob, Abigail Child, $12.00

CYMK, Michael Coffey, $14.00

Debts and Obligations, Alicia Cohen, $12.00

Moira, Norma Cole, $12.00

It Then, Danielle Collobert, $10.00

Parcel, Sarah Anne Cox, $12.00

Lapses, John Crouse, $10.00

Headlines, John Crouse, $12.00

The Arcades, Michael Davidson, $12.00

Candor, Alan Davies, $10.00

iduna, kari edwards, $12.00

Rome, A Mobile Home, Jerry Estrin, Roof Books and Potes & Poets with O Books, $9.00

Turn Left in Order to Go Right, Norman Fischer, $12.00

Time Rations, Benjamin Friedlander, $12.00

Startle Response, Heather Fuller, $12.00

byt, William Fuller, $12.00

The Sugar Borders, William Fuller, $12.00

DeathStar/Ricochet, Judith Goldman, $14.00

War and Peace 2, edited by Judith Goldman and Leslie Scalapino, $14.00

War and Peace 3, edited by Judith Goldman and Leslie Scalapino, $14.00

Phantom Anthems, Robert Grenier, $12.00

What I Believe   Transpiration/Transpiring   Minnesota, Robert Grenier, $24.00

The Inveterate Life, Jessica Grim, $12.00

Fray, Jessica Grim, $12.00

Music or Forgetting, E. Tracy Grinnell, $12.00

Some Clear Souvenir, E. Tracy Grinnell, $12.00

Memory Play, Carla Harryman, $9.00

The Words/after Carl Sandburg's Rootabaga Stories and Jean-Paul Sartre, Carla Harryman, $12.00

The Quietist, Fanny Howe, $9.00

Around Sea, Brenda Iijima, $12.00

VEL, P. Inman, $12.00

60 lv Bo(e)mbs, Paolo Javier, $12.00

The History of the Loma People, Paul D. Korvah, $12.00

248 mgs., a panic picnic, Susan Landers, $12.00

Covers, Susan Landers, $12.00

Curve, Andrew Levy, $12.00

Values Chauffeur You, Andrew Levy, $12.00

Dreaming Close By, Rick London, $12.00

Abjections, Rick London, $5.00

Dissuasion Crowds the Slow Worker, Lori Lubeski, $10.00

Containment Scenario, M. Mara-Ann, $15.00

Plum Stones: Cartoons of No Heaven, Michael McClure, $13.00

The Case, Laura Moriarty, $12.00

Home on the Range (The Night Sky with Stars in My Mouth), Tenney Nathanson, $12.00

Criteria, Sianne Ngai, $11.00

Close to me & Closer . . . (The Language of Heaven) and Désamère, Alice Notley, $14.00

Catenary Odes, Ted Pearson, $12.00

Collision Center, Randall Potts, $12.00

Light, Jerry Ratch, $12.00

(where late the sweet) BIRDS SANG, Stephen Ratcliffe, $12.00

Tottering State, Tom Raworth, $15.00

Visible Shivers, Tom Raworth, (Out of Print)

Kismet, Pat Reed, $12.00

Cold Heaven, Camille Roy, $12.00

The Seven Voices, Lisa Samuels, $12.00

Crowd and not evening or light, Leslie Scalapino, $12.00

Enough, an anthology edited by Leslie Scalapino and Rick London, $16.00

O ONE/AN ANTHOLOGY ed. Leslie Scalapino, $12.00

O TWO/AN ANTHOLOGY: What is the inside, what is outside?, ed. Leslie Scalapino, $12.00

O/4: Subliminal Time, ed. Leslie Scalapino, $12.00

War and Peace, ed. Leslie Scalapino, $14.00

The India Book: Essays and Translations, Andrew Schelling, $12.00

" . . . But I Couldn't Speak . . .", Jono Schneider, $12.00

Rumors of Buildings To Live In, Keith Shein, $12.00

A's Dream, Aaron Shurin, $12.00

In Memory of My Theories, Rod Smith, $12.00

Partisans, Rodrigo Toscano, $12.00

Lilyfoil, Elizabeth Treadwell, $12.00

trespasses, Padcha Tuntha-Obas, $12.00

Homing Devices, Liz Waldner, $12.00

Picture of The Picture of The Image in The Glass, Craig Watson, $12.00